This book is given with the
compliments of B Hollowell & Son
Funeral Directors to give help in
arranging the funeral of a loved one

When We Remember

Inspiration & Integrity for a Meaningful Funeral

Melissa Abraham

Melissa Abraham
B.Mus.Ed., L.T.C.L., MACE

When We Remember:
Inspiration and Integrity for a Meaningful Funeral

Published by:
Three Things Pty Ltd
45 Emma St, Mona Vale
NSW 2103 Australia

Three Things Pty Ltd

www.3thingz.com

1. Funeral Service – Handbooks, manuals, etc
2. Death care industry – Planning
3. Death care industry

265.85

1. Funeral rites and ceremonies
2. Mourning Etiquette
3. Death – Handbooks, manuals, etc.

741.994

Cover photograph by Jostein Hauge **www.incredipix.com**
Other Photography sourced from **www.bigstockphoto.com** and **www.istockphoto.com**
Layout and Design by GoDesign **www.GoDesign.net.au**
Printed and bound in China

ISBN 978-0-9803510-0-2

Thankyou

So many people have given so freely of their time, expertise, emotional energy and plain old encouragement. Everybody seemed to instinctively recognise the importance of the project, and I am forever grateful for your generosity of spirit.

For wise counsel, uncompromising support and generous sharing of experience –

Jenny Alexander, Lana Allison, Lyn Anderson, Timur Arutyunyan, Michelle Clendining, Penny Coucil, John & Rosie Cox, Susan Dado, Tonia Davies, Ann Dorey, Gill Evans, Dr Chris Farmer, Trevor Francis-Jones, Rob Goode, Scott Harris, Alexey Kornilov, Larry McCabe, Nikita Obukhov, Regula Odermatt, Rosemary Osborne, Lydia Pearson, Dr Frank Quinn, Rev John Reid, Fabian Reisner, Jan Siering, Luiz Sena, Alan Smith, Nikki Smith, Peter Stewart fms, Alan Stokes, Ian Strathie, Steve Wright, the Very Rev John Young.

Songs of praise to the magnificent music team –

Jim Abraham, Ross A'hern, Dr Carlos Alvarado, Karen Ashworth, Daniel Barnett, Elaine Beckett, Michael Bennett, Daniel Brown, Brad Child, Greg Crittendon, Iva Davies, Jane Hennessy, Simon Leadley, Leah Lock, Alexandra Loukianova, LVS Choir, Manly-Warringah Choir, Michelle Ollson, Rosemary Osborne, Robert Pearce, Lionel Robinson, Tim Ryan, Lorraine Silk, Verity Snook, Murilo Tanouye, Sue Taylor, Antonia Todorova, Brydon Stace, Dan Walker, Steve Watson, Ami Williamson, Andrew Wilson, Naira Yusofova.

At the business end of making things actually happen –

Emerson Brantley, Jennifer Harris, William Inglis, Karen McCreadie, Lyle McNeish, Nigel Walker, Tim Yuan, Jean Zhu, Trackdown Studios, all the incredible team at Melbourne IT and a special mention to Rob Baker at GoDesign.net.au for beautifully efficient graphic design, and for sharing the vision for the project from the very early stages!

Dedicated to

The unknown person at Loquat Valley
who slipped a note into my handbag that simply read...

"We were with you in your happiness
and we are still with you now"

With love to the two people that confirmed
my faith in the importance of the project
'When We Remember'

Nellie Anderson nee Jurd (27 June 1912 – 17 March 2006)
Frank Clendining (29 December 1936 – 2 March 2007)

And of course to my irreplaceable, wise, patient
and unwaveringly loving husband

Jim

"To love is to take the greatest risk of all.
It is to place one's future and one's happiness into another's hands.
It is to allow oneself to trust without reserve.
It is to accept vulnerability.
And thus I love you."

Helen Thompson (1943 -)

Chapter 1 Introduction

If you are reading this book because you are planning the funeral of a loved one, I sincerely hope that you receive some comfort and help from the pages within.

While our intelligence is not diminished by grief, our ability to make clear, considered decisions can be. Often it is difficult to think of all the things that need to be done whilst feeling so vulnerable and distressed. As a result, details are missed, choices are rushed, and regret only serves to compound the sadness as time goes by.

'When We Remember' has been created to help prepare and support families under the pressure of time. Guidance has been generously offered from individuals, families, psychologists, religious leaders, secular celebrants and Funeral Directors.

This easy to use reference guide covers everything you may need to consider, from the first few hours, to all the elements of designing a fitting tribute, to resources for helping you to come to terms with your loss.

Perhaps the death of your loved one has been sudden. Or perhaps you are preparing for the death of someone you love. You will find a wealth of information that you may not have considered. It is advised that you leave this book and CD in an accessible place, and read it when you feel ready. You may find you read the entire book, or decide only one or two sections are relevant – the choice is yours.

If you are reading this with a view to arranging your own tribute then you can be assured of a heartfelt thankyou from family and friends. It is a true act of love to relieve the burden at a time when many may be too distressed to think clearly, and your thoughtfulness will be greatly appreciated.

If we are lucky life is full of great events; a wedding, the birth of a child, buying our first home, starting a new career. Each takes many months or even years in the planning. These events are openly discussed with friends and family, magazines and countless websites cover every detail. Yet when it comes to death, there is often only silence as we each struggle to come to terms with the loss in our own way.

My hope is that **'When We Remember'** will help to break that taboo so that we may honour and cherish a life well lived. And at the same time help make the lives of those left behind a little easier.

Meaningful Funerals

Although many people will thankfully only be responsible for organising one or two funerals in their lifetime, they will probably attend many more.

As a result, when it comes time to plan a tribute most people assume it should be like the ones they have attended previously, but this need not be the case.

We are all different. It follows therefore that these differences should be acknowledged and celebrated when we farewell a loved one.

Personalising a final tribute, no matter how small the detail, can be a powerful help in satisfying our human need to make sense of what we cannot control.

"This was not just anybody's funeral; it was my Peter's funeral. We honoured him well, and he was just as present in our hearts & minds as he was before he died."

The journey through grief may take some time, and it is important to recognise the signposts as we pass them along the way.

> A funeral or memorial ritual is a vital first checkpoint – the moment we openly acknowledge our loss, our vulnerability, and our need to recreate a new future.

Guidance

There are many experienced professionals available to you. Although decisions are yours, you are not alone. We are guided and supported by the presence of others.

Comfort

We take comfort in long-held traditions or find strong purpose in creating new ones. Your journey is unique, but you are surrounded by people that will want to help you.

Reassurance

We are reassured that we are moving *through* grief, and understand that we will not always feel this way.

Some things are timeless, but modern living brings its own set of challenges.

We live in a time now that gives unprecedented opportunity for travel, information exchange, cultural awareness, experimentation and questioning of belief.

We have broken with tradition in many areas of life and our expectations are different.

We live longer, medical advances have seen huge leaps in life expectancy, yet death is an inevitable part of living and will come to us all eventually.

Funerals often take place in the first week after somebody dies and for many people this is still very much a period of shock and unreality. We are usually so unprepared.

Death is not optional, and hiding from the reality will not make it go away. When people do not move well through grief, a grief counsellor or other professional may need to help through recreating meaningful rituals and acknowledging the loss in the reality of our daily lives.

Beliefs

If you have a strong spiritual belief or cultural tradition, then you have valuable armour to shield and strengthen you in the time ahead.

Companions

If you have a good network of family or friends, call on them often.

Experiences

If you have outlived many others, then you will know that grief is a journey; that we can and do move forward in time. Our futures may be different to the ones we had imagined, but we can create new hopes and find new purpose to our days ahead.

How to use this resource

Use as much or as little information as you need. Perhaps mark passages that are relevant or meaningful to you. Sometimes we can become overwhelmed with information and choice, or forget ideas that we really wanted to include in a tribute.

The enclosed CD provides many more options, and is also valuable by itself to provide comfort in the time ahead.

Make your options as clear and simple as possible. Keep a record of your decisions. Laugh, cry, imagine, think, pray, mourn, love and remember.

- The beginning of this book covers the first hours after somebody dies.

- The second section looks at the first few days and the important decisions that need to be made at this time.

- The third and largest section of this book offers options for creating a meaningful funeral.

- The fourth section looks at the weeks and months following a funeral.

It is hoped that you will find inspiration, support and clarity in the following pages.

Chapter 2 The First Few Hours

> It is a sad but absolute truth that life and death are always partners. One must follow the other.

Some deaths are expected, some are not. No matter how much notice we are given, we are never fully prepared for the reality of the death of a loved one.

We are all different. Every person, every relationship, every circumstance, every belief will be part of the unique experience that you have at this time.

Sometimes our previous experiences with death will provide great comfort, and at other times our past losses will only feel closer to hand.

You may find that you are very calm, especially if you have been able to care for somebody well in the time leading up to an expected death. When first faced with the news, it is possible to feel only love, peace and thankfulness for having shared love with someone. You will of course feel sadness in the moments ahead that you miss their physical presence, but please do not assume that all deaths are filled only with sorrow.

You may feel emotions that surprise you. Shock will play its hand in many ways – you could feel anything from acceptance to complete numbness and disbelief, through to complete breakdown and loss of control.

When first faced with death, every one of our reactions is considered normal.

If the death of a loved one is completely unexpected and unprepared for, then you will need to accept that it will take time for the new reality to sink in.

Our brains and bodies are wonderfully designed to cope with stress in many ways, and you will need to accept every one of your emotions as they rise and fall in the days ahead.

Please be sure to contact close friends and family for support. This is a time of accepting help, of being flexible in your expectations of others and yourself, and understanding that we are all vulnerable. Let people help you.

Talk, touch and hug, laugh, cry, be childlike, be emotional, be strong at times if you must, but take each hour and day one at a time. Accept each moment exactly as it is.

Grief is a journey,
not a destination.

As you travel through the next few days, there are many decisions to be made and you will probably find that you are not able to concentrate as you would like.

There is a logical way forward, and each step along the way has a variety of things to consider and decisions to be made.

"Losing my father was so just different to when we lost Helen.

One death we were prepared for – we had months of sharing precious moments and in the end we all knew that it was just the way of things.

We cried and grieved, but we also laughed... it was sad yet it was also ok somehow.

But when Helen went – the shock was so overwhelming. Nobody could believe it. Nobody was prepared. How can you prepare for something like that?"

Start at the beginning, and move through the process of each stage. Information is given a piece at a time and decisions will be made in turn.

You do not have to deal with everything all at once – in fact your thoughts will become clearer and more in tune with your individual needs as time passes.

What to Do When Somebody Dies

At Home

If a person dies naturally at home and has been attended by a doctor in the previous three months, it is not necessary to have them removed immediately.

You will need to contact your doctor and your choice of Funeral Director. Most Funeral Directors are available 24 hours and can provide excellent support when your doctor cannot be easily reached. They will listen to your needs, giving you support and guidance in what to do next.

In Hospital

If a person dies in hospital, the staff will be able to take care of initial arrangements and can often contact the Funeral Director of your choice for you.

All hospitals, hospices and other place of care will always do their very best to support you at this time. Many will have certain rooms set aside for families to gather. Even if the hospital you are in is a very busy one, please do not feel that you are "in the way". Take your time; accept help and offers of support. The health profession is staffed by people that have a very clear understanding of the things you may be feeling at this moment.

Unusual Circumstances

If a person dies unexpectedly, by accident, in a public place or in unusual circumstances, then certain government agencies will need to be informed. Your Funeral Director will be involved and will be able to give advice on what to expect and how to proceed.

Sometimes we are completely unprepared for someone to die, and this shock adds to the grief to create a more complex set of emotions.

You may be guided by many trained people, including police, ambulance staff, doctors, nurses, clergy, Funeral Directors and other professionals.

When a death occurs in an unexpected way or in unusual circumstances, it is important to take one step at a time.

Try not to look too far ahead.

Try to have others around you so that information can be recalled by both of you.

Try to write down any important information you are given.

Be patient with the processes and yourself.

What Happens First?

Support

If you are alone, contact your close support group.

One or two trusted friends or relatives will be absolutely invaluable at this time. Do not make decisions alone, unless the death was expected and had been prepared for.

Care

Care of the deceased person's body will be organised.

At some stage the deceased person's body will need to be transferred or transported. This is usually from the place of death to the Funeral Director's premises, and then again at a later stage for committal of the body to a final resting place.

It is very important that you understand there is no urgent rush to immediately transport somebody when they have died. Although each circumstance will be different, do not feel pressured to make an instant decision on your choice of Funeral Director or any of the decisions that will follow in the next few hours.

Certificate

A doctor must prepare a Medical Certificate stating the Cause of Death. If the doctor has not attended the deceased in the last three months, or if the doctor is uncertain as to the exact cause of death, then the certification must be referred to the Coroner or other government agencies.

Meaningful Tribute

Start to consider the options available for choosing a final resting place, and how best to respect and remember the person that has died.

This last sentence is not to be taken lightly – in fact it is the basis of this entire book. As you begin through the next few days, be aware that you will be faced with many decisions. It is possible to hand over these decisions completely to others. Or perhaps you will try to keep total control yourself.

If at all possible, find a compromise. Use others to carry out your personal wishes. Use their skills and experience to compliment your knowledge of the person that has died.

Craft a meaningful experience that has integrity for both the person that has died and for those who remain.

Chapter 3 How Will the Funeral Director Help?

The role of your Funeral Director is to represent you and your family with absolute integrity, respect and discretion at all times.

Many people may feel uncomfortable talking about the responsibilities and tasks of a Funeral Director. Some people would rather not know the details, and others feel that respect for the deceased should extend to keeping a respectful distance from those that work in the death-care industry.

Because death is perhaps one of society's last taboos, Funeral Directors are generally not able to discuss their work-day lives freely.

The result of all this can be that when faced with the death of a loved one, some people are very uncomfortable or nervous when first meeting with their Funeral Director.

Perhaps they are unsure what will happen, or what to ask for, or they may not understand the range of choices that are available to them. Some people may feel embarrassed to ask for what they really want, while others may feel helplessly swept along by events, unable to find their true voice.

Funeral Directors are very experienced in helping you come to suitable decisions in planning a funeral. They may have solutions to problems, or can often suggest alternatives to consider.

Sometimes we need Funeral Directors to act as a go-between for different groups in our family. Sometimes we need extra emotional or practical help to get decisions finalised.

As coordinators of a very important day, Funeral Directors take on a huge amount of responsibility and will often work on tasks for people for many hours beyond what was expected, to ensure that the day runs as smoothly as possible.

They are highly aware of the significance of their work, and will do whatever they can to ensure families are fully supported throughout the entire experience.

Thankfully some people are drawn to the work of a Funeral Director, and even talk about their decision to work in this field as a powerful calling or life choice.

Funeral Directors seek the opportunity to profoundly assist people in a time of need, and they are returned with great emotional, social and spiritual rewards for this life of service.

Pre-Arranged Services

Perhaps you are reading this book while considering your own funeral arrangements.

Funeral Directors are very experienced in assisting people to record their plans and preferences. They can help you with practical information, suggestions, and many other relevant ideas and services.

The procedure can be as simple or detailed as you desire.

Your Funeral Director will accept responsibility for ensuring, as closely as possible, that your wishes are carried out. When the time comes they can quietly and efficiently attend to all necessary arrangements, causing no disruption to grieving loved ones.

Once you have decided on your Funeral Director, many people choose to take the next step and pre-pay for their funeral. In many areas it is a government requirement that your funds are invested in a security guaranteed manner, and therefore your investment is protected well ahead of the time it is needed.

Understandably, this takes a great load off the grieving family and friends. Loved ones are given the opportunity to mourn their loss without having the additional stress of arranging the funeral.

Some benefits in pre-paying your funeral include –

Financial

Taking the financial worry off the shoulders of your loved ones.

Organisation

Greatly reducing the amount of time your family will need to spend on administrative matters.

Focus on Family

Increasing the time your family will have to gather together at this very important and often difficult time.

Comfort

You will be reassuring your family that you were prepared. Your acceptance will hopefully assist your family to find peace in the days following your passing.

How Do We Select a Funeral Director?

Accreditation

There are many unifying professional associations throughout the industry that can provide price guidelines, working practices and other legal requirements, together with mediation services or a system for reporting complaints about members should a problem arise during or after a funeral.

To be part of such an association, a Funeral Director and their staff and premises must meet standards of skills, facilities and procedures, ethics, and government compliance.

Be sure that your Funeral Director is part of such an association.

Recommendation

Personal recommendation from trusted friends and colleagues is a good way to ensure that you receive the style and quality of service you want.

Many families may have a tradition of service with a particular Funeral Director. If you relatively new to an area, a personal recommendation from a trusted local can be a great help.

Comparison

Telephone and visit some Funeral Directors in your area. Ensure that they are an accredited member of an association, and get a written quote if you know the goods and services you would like. Perhaps discuss matters with friends and family, to decide if the Funeral Director's services and premises are a good match for your needs.

It is possible that you may have difficulty selecting a Funeral Director. You may be so overwhelmed with different emotions, or even in denial about having to deal with the situation at all.

If you are feeling this way, then the difficulty may be not with the choice, but within you. This is why it's a good idea to take someone with you, preferably someone that will be able to offer some objectivity and help you reach a decision.

Ensure that a Funeral Director is part of an association, and get a written quote. If the cost is acceptable simply go ahead and employ their services.

The next few days will challenge you emotionally and mentally, with many more decisions to be made. Trust that you and your family will be taken care of.

What Will the Funeral Director Do?

The role of your Funeral Director is to represent you and your family with absolute integrity, respect and discretion at all times.

They are very experienced in dealing with an incredible variety of situations surrounding death, and can provide excellent guidance for you and the individual members of your family during this vulnerable and emotional period.

Funeral Directors should provide support and an environment of calm reassurance, for you and your family to work within for the first few days following the death of a loved one.

They should be able to assist you in all matters at this time, and will know the people to refer you to if they themselves cannot help.

Practical Care

Often the first task a Funeral Director will have is to transport and care for the body of the person that has died.

Once you have appointed your Funeral Director they can act on your behalf to ensure suitable arrangements are made.

They will also become the first port of call for any government agencies that may be involved following an unexpected death, helping you to complete any administrative matters.

Consultation

Your Funeral Director will meet with you to discuss the immediate decisions, covered in detail in the next section of this book.

This meeting is usually for an hour or more and should take place as early as reasonably possible, certainly within the first 24 or 48 hours.

It is often able to be held at a venue you find most comfortable, either at your home or at the Funeral Director's premises.

You may wish to ensure that more than one person attends the meeting. It can be quite difficult absorb information at this time.

Paperwork

There are certain legal requirements when somebody dies and your Funeral Director will ensure that these are met.

In addition to a Cause of Death Certificate issued by the doctor, every death will need to be registered at the appropriate government department. There may be additional documentation required for cremation and burial.

Most Funeral Directors will ensure that you are given multiple copies of certificates, as you will need these later on when dealing with banks and other personal matters.

Coordinator

Use your Funeral Director as a "Personal Assistant" or Coordinator.

Aside from their obvious experience and expertise in an area of life most of us know very little about, Funeral Directors can play a pivotal role in assisting you to grieve in a healthy manner.

While it can certainly be good to keep busy at this difficult time, it is important that you devote your limited energy toward the things that only you and your family can do best.

Only your close friends and family can ensure that you create a meaningful and memorable experience for all who remain when somebody dies.

You will need to consider the relationships, interests and beliefs of your loved one. Respect for them will combine with the feelings of those that mourn, and slowly but surely a worthwhile and individual farewell will take shape.

Funeral Directors will have experience and be skilled in organising funerals for many and varied religious or spiritual belief backgrounds.

Your Funeral Director can provide many services personally for you – these may include staff to greet and care for all your family and other mourners, venue coordination, transport, sometimes recorded music and literature library, and so on.

They can advise on suitable services and goods, for example flowers, singers, celebrants, and grief counsellors.

> Funeral Directors will ensure that whenever possible your wishes are met, and may have very useful suggestions that you may not have considered.

How Much Will It All Cost?

The cost of a funeral can generally be divided into three main areas –

Professional Fees

Fees for the services of the Funeral Director, their staff and their premises.

These are often fixed at a base rate, and then added to if extra services are required. Extra services should be quoted and may include items such as embalming, special arrangements with transport, international transfer or burial, and other considerations.

Disbursements

The fees that must be paid, or are paid for on your behalf.

As part of their professional service, your Funeral Director can coordinate and pay for the many items and services that may be required.

Some examples include fees for the certifying doctor, Death Certificates and other government requirements, the church or celebrant, flowers, musicians, catering, newspaper obituaries and other printing for the funeral.

Once these are paid for by the Funeral Director, you are then obliged to reimburse them. You should be kept fully informed of non-essential arrangements.

The Coffin and Corresponding Committal

Burial or Cremation

Both burial and cremation require that a coffin or container be used, and there are health and safety laws governing the choice and construction of materials.

With so many variations in services and options, it is important to get itemised quotes.

Do consider carefully the amount of money that you will commit to. Although you will want to show respect and honour the deceased, they would certainly not want you to add financial difficulty to your grief in the months ahead.

The financial costs will be clearly outlined in writing, including estimates of any optional goods or services you may be considering.

In many countries this is a clear legal requirement for all licensed Funeral Directors and their premises.

Certainly it is always good sense in any situation to have written quotes, and the employment of the services of a Funeral Director is no different.

With many of the goods and services there will be a range of costs and choices offered to you.

If you have a budget, it can be very useful to let the Funeral Director know at the beginning of a meeting. It can be upsetting and a waste of your time to discuss options for items that you are not able to afford at this time.

Try to balance your need to honour the passing of a loved one with your immediate financial situation, especially if a death has been unexpected. It may seem that nothing is more important at this time, or that money is meaningless and not even a consideration when planning a funeral and interment.

Take a little time to discuss your choices with others, and find the financial balance that is right for your and your family, both now and in the months to come.

Be sure to inform the Funeral Director and seek advice if you are planning to rely on the estate or will of the person that has died to finance a funeral.

In some legal systems this money may not be available for several weeks or even months. Be especially aware if shares or property needs to be sold – it is usually not possible to release this money until the proper legal processes have been completed.

Some countries will allow the Funeral Director to submit to the bank a single account for the total of all goods and services. This money will be released to the Funeral Director to cover their own fees, and the disbursements they have already paid on your behalf.

Ensure that you receive a written quote from the first meeting, and that you are fully informed of the cost of any optional item that you request at a later date.

In Summary

There is a logical way forward when somebody dies. You will be assisted by many professionals along the way, and should always enlist and accept the support of your close friends and family.

Shock will play a part in the first few days, and you should not be surprised by any emotion you feel. When first faced with death, every one of our reactions may be considered normal.

As the hours and moments pass, you will feel many emotions and have to deal with a large number of decisions. Take one step at a time. Understand you will not always feel this way.

Unless you are very well prepared beforehand, you will need to use the services of a Funeral Director. They are specialists with a wealth of experience in caring for the deceased person, your family, and the legal requirements at this time.

Use Funeral Directors to deal with practicalities while you devote your energies to that which only you and your family can do.

If necessary, select your Funeral Director through –

- Recommendation from a National Association of Funeral Directors
- Comparison by visiting several in your area
- Personal recommendation from trusted friends and colleagues

Ensure that you receive a written quote from the first meeting, and that you are fully informed of the cost of any optional item that you request at a later date.

Take this opportunity to reflect and create a meaningful tribute for a loved one. Gather together, reinforce that all that was shared still remains, nothing that was said is now unsaid, nothing that was done is now undone.

Start a new relationship, in memory.
Reinforce your lives together.
Be supported by others around you.
Do your best to accept what you have been given.

When you are going through grief, just be sure to keep going.
This, too, shall pass.

Chapter 4 The First Decisions

The next three chapters deal with the practical decisions that need to be made in the first day or two following the death of a loved one.

It is always a relief for a family to carry out the wishes of somebody who has left instructions for their own funeral and interment.

Unfortunately many people find themselves, at a time of crisis, having to use their "best" judgement. Making arrangements for the funeral of a loved one can be a time of having to think very carefully, at a time when you are often least able to.

Respect the integrity and memory of the person who has died

Allow meaningful experiences for those who remain

You may already have a very clear idea on what you plan to do. Or you may be completely unprepared and overwhelmed, especially if you have never organised a funeral before.

Below is a brief outline of some of your choices –

Please notice that the choice of burial or cremation is only a part of the process. Regardless of which method you prefer there are still many possibilities to create meaningful experiences and memories.

Before	Viewing Funeral Other gatherings or observances
At Cremation or Burial	Service or other rituals
After	Memorial Service Wake or informal gathering Placing of headstone or plaque Scattering of ashes Other memorial activity

Religious or other personal beliefs will usually dictate whether cremation or burial is the most suitable choice.

Some people have very strong views regarding this choice. For others it is not something they have really considered, and they are not really sure what the implications or issues are.

Sometimes people leave written instructions with a will, regarding cremation or burial. If there is doubt it is always worth contacting the person's solicitor to check if instructions have been left. It may be possible for the family to be advised of any written instructions left by a person, without involving a complete reading of a will. This is an important option to consider, as it would be very difficult to discover too late that a person's final wishes were not carried out.

By the same token, it is very important to discuss any firmly held beliefs with those close to you. If written instructions have been left then others can only be expected to follow them if they are aware that the instructions exist.

It may not always be financially possible to follow someone's last wishes. Sometimes it may not be possible at all, due to the unforeseen circumstances of the death.

You may seek advice from family, close friends and the professionals that you are in contact with at this time. Their counsel and concern will help support any decisions you make. Professionals have experience and compassion that may help find solutions that you have not considered.

You may feel pressured by time and your strong desire to do the right thing. It can be very difficult to keep a balanced perspective during a time of grief.

Trust that you will do the best you can, in the circumstances that you are given.

Burial

For many religions and spiritual beliefs, burial is the traditional choice.

Some people feel that it is the most fitting way to lay a loved one to rest, and there are often long-held rituals and symbols that may accompany a burial. Some religions and cultures strictly require burial; in other countries and cultures only burial is possible.

A burial will require a burial site, almost always in a community designated cemetery.

Sometimes these cemeteries are privately owned, and in some circumstances it is even possible to bury a loved one on privately owned land. Remember that privately owned land can be sold or transferred, and you may wish to check whether a legally binding arrangement has been set up to prevent this in the years to come.

Perhaps there is a pre-purchased site or an obvious choice with regard to family tradition. If so then your decisions are made a little easier, and your Funeral Director will be able to advise you on the remaining procedures.

It is becoming increasing popular to consider burial in a natural setting. New burial sites are being established where instead of a large headstone being placed, a tree or other plants are encouraged.

If you wish to have a burial and need to wait for a period of time before friends and family can gather, then you may need to consider embalming. There are also certain medical and other circumstances when embalming is considered necessary.

If a person has died while travelling or living in another country, it may not be possible to return them for burial. There are many laws governing the international transport of somebody that has died, and depending on the circumstances and countries involved, these regulations may not be able to be met.

Do not be discouraged if this situation arises. You may need to consider cremation in the county that the person died, and then transporting the ashes for burial.

Your plans for remembrance services and memorials with family and friends can remain as meaningful as ever.

Cremation

Some world religions have always preferred cremation to burial. Cremation is certainly growing in popularity, and in some areas more than half of all families will request cremation. This is particularly true in city areas, where cremation facilities are readily available.

Cremation is usually not acceptable within Orthodox Judaism, Islam and Eastern Orthodoxy. However, most Christian denominations approve of cremation, and it is the preferred method among Hindus and many Buddhists.

An example of changing beliefs can be found in the Roman Catholic Church. It is now generally considered that Christian cremation does not deny the resurrection of the body, immortality of the soul, and the existence of eternal life.

The Catholic Church does recommend cremated remains are disposed of in a way that indicates respect for the body of the deceased person, and a memorial in a public place allows the deceased person's commitment to Christianity to still be proclaimed.

If you do not follow a conventional religious faith, you will still have beliefs of your own that may affect your decision. There are many reasons why an individual may or may not choose cremation.

You may feel that not having a burial is denying the reality of death, that it is necessary to watch a coffin being lowered into the ground to fully accept someone's passing.

Or you may feel the opposite – that a cremation acknowledges the reality that the person is no longer inhabiting their body, that their spirit has long since departed.

Some people have said that they feel a cremation is somehow "more final" than a burial. This may be related to beliefs held in ancient times, such as the period of the Egyptian pyramids, when nobility were preserved and then entombed with personal possessions that may be useful to them in the after-life.

In addition to religious and personal beliefs, there are other matters to consider. For example, a cremation can give much greater opportunity for placing ashes in a location that has personal meaning.

A cremation may cost less than a burial, although this is not always the case.

Following cremation the ashes will be returned to you in a pre-chosen container or urn. There are now some interesting and creative ideas regarding the use of ashes in providing a permanent memorial, including jewellery or other objects. Many crematoriums will also scatter ashes for you on their grounds if this is your instruction.

Whether you opt for burial or cremation, there are still many possibilities to create meaningful experiences and memories.

Often people will opt for cremation with no accompanying funeral or gathering in an attempt to avoid the pain of grief. It doesn't work that way.

How and where you choose to commit the body of someone that has died is only one part of a journey that will take quite some time to travel.

We all need to mark the death of a loved one with the respect, through action, that such a significant event deserves – creating meaningful memories that will only become more important in the weeks and months ahead. It is part of the healing process.

Embalming

Embalming is a skilled process where a person's body fluids are replaced with agents that greatly slow the degeneration of the body.

Some people are in favour of embalming as it can maintain a person's appearance, and can assist if a funeral or interment cannot take place quickly.

Other people reject embalming as interference with a natural process, and will choose to commit somebody quickly rather than wait for all family and friends to gather from across the lands.

Refrigeration is often all that is required if a funeral and the following burial or cremation will occur reasonably quickly.

Your Funeral Director can advise you further on whether embalming is considered necessary or desirable in your family's particular circumstance.

> We were just so unprepared for it. Who looks at a 20 year old and wonders what arrangements he would want? We just had to remember that he was part of our family, and he would be happy with our decisions.

Caskets and Coffins

A casket or coffin must be used for a viewing, for transport, and for both cremation and burial. A person will be buried in their coffin, and people remain in their coffin for the cremation process.

There are many possibilities and personal opinions regarding the type of coffin used.

For some families it may be of great importance that a loved one is shown respect by providing the finest level of quality in materials and fittings for a coffin. This is often extended to the type of memorial that is placed as well.

Some people are dedicated to providing inexpensive and environmentally friendly options, including the use of heavy duty "cardboard", sustainable resources such as bamboo, or even home-made wooden alternatives. Please be aware that these arrangements almost always need to be made in advance, and that there are health and safety guidelines that must be adhered to.

Your Funeral Director can be an excellent source of information regarding the legal requirements for transport and committal either through burial or cremation.

A casket or coffin will form a significant part of the total cost of a funeral.

Sometimes people can lose perspective over the importance of this choice.

Please do not feel pressured into making decisions that will cause financial difficulties for those that remain living. Ask your Funeral Director for alternatives, consult with family and friends, and if necessary delay your decision for 24 hours or more. The last thing a deceased loved one would want is for those that are left to have added pressure in the months ahead.

Some people will be completely comfortable in providing the best coffin they can reasonably manage, and may even ask for handles or small metal fixtures to be returned to them as a reminder of sharing the process of death with their loved one.

Coffins may have items placed on them or sometimes in them prior to committal. If cremation is chosen then you will need to check with the Funeral Director regarding the suitability of certain objects, for example a favourite toy or a piece of jewellery. Some people have even decorated the actual coffin itself with specific reminders of a person's interests or personality.

Viewing

A viewing is simply the opportunity to see the deceased once they have been placed in a coffin.

Although a very personal choice, many people who have opted for a viewing speak gratefully and very positively of the opportunity to see their loved one again and better understand the reality of death.

Too often we are encouraged to be strong, to talk in hushed tones or use words that simplify or deny the major impact of death.

We are used to seeing symbols for happiness, for love, for financial success, for many other publicly acceptable milestones and events in our lives. The media and people in our daily lives encourage us to share these important experiences.

Yet when faced with the death of a loved one, one of the most profoundly moving experiences we will ever have, we can sometimes feel isolated and almost encouraged to withdraw and mourn silently and privately alone.

When we have a viewing we understand with our physical senses the reality of death, and the ultimate symbol of death is always the dead body itself.

I thought it would be shocking, I was worried that I would be more upset and unable to cope. In fact the opposite occurred. She just looked so peaceful, I found myself just smiling and wishing her all the love that she had given me over the years.

At that exact moment I understood two things very clearly – I knew she was gone, and I somehow also knew that I would be alright.

In general, Western society can learn much from other cultures, especially those that embrace death as a natural part of life. Death is not optional, it will happen to us all eventually.

If a person dies in your presence at home or elsewhere, spending some time in their company can give much needed space for final conversation and goodbye. It therefore follows that if you were not present when they died, you may well need to do exactly the same thing.

If you are to have a viewing, children should not be excluded as a matter of course. With preparation as to what they might expect, the experience can be very useful for children to understand what has happened.

Children are often very influenced by their parents, so be mindful to really listen to what they want rather than assume they don't want to be involved. Viewing can help bring closure for children just as it can for adults, and assist in their healing journey.

Some religions and cultures, such as the traditional Irish culture, embrace viewing the body of a deceased person wholeheartedly, and it can form a central part of the grieving experience.

Others such as the Aboriginal Australian culture shun the idea, believing it is important to see the person only while alive. It is believed to take away their spirit and is considered disrespectful to view the deceased.

Of course no mourner should ever be forced to take part, and the phrase "for your own good" is quite irrelevant at this time. We all grieve in different ways, and a reluctant or unwanted memory can have long lasting negative effects.

If a person has died of an accident or other misfortune that has left them disfigured, then you may need to discuss a decision to have a viewing with your Funeral Director and other professionals.

Some people will still wish to go ahead, feeling that their imaginings of a traumatic death will haunt them more than the reality. It may be possible to arrange a viewing so as to minimise the distress where possible.

Memorials

Regardless of whether a burial or cremation is chosen, decisions regarding a visible memorial do not have to be made immediately.

There are so many practical decisions that must be made in the first few days, and deciding on appropriate wording, styles and themes for a memorial is usually best left for a later time.

You may initially decide on a very grand memorial, or no visible memorial at all. In the days and weeks ahead, this decision can alter dramatically as perspective returns and you are able to consider more easily the meaningfulness of a memorial.

Once ordered, it will usually take many weeks to prepare your chosen memorial.

The occasion of scattering ashes or placing a memorial can give an excellent opportunity for people to gather again in the weeks or months following death, when the initial sting of grief has subsided.

It can give people another chance to reflect, both personally and as a group, on the reality of someone's passing and what this means to those that are left.

Many people feel that they are not in "real time" at the time of a funeral. If you choose to meet when a memorial is placed, this further opportunity to express your love and reflections can be an excellent way of moving forward.

A gathering could occur on a monthly anniversary of the death, or at significant dates such as birthdays and other special occasions.

Cremation and Memorials

Choosing cremation will offer more choices regarding a loved one's final resting place. Many crematoriums and cemeteries offer a variety of options for interment or scattering of ashes. These can include burial of ashes in a small plot or garden, or placement in a wall, or simply scattering ashes in a memorial garden.

Depending on the personality and beliefs of the person who has died, it can be very appropriate to erect a memorial plaque at one location and scatter ashes at another, more meaningful location.

Some people feel strongly about returning ashes freely to the natural world, perhaps over water or in a familiar place of natural beauty or special significance.

If you wish to scatter ashes in a public place, there are legal requirements to consider and your Funeral Director can advise you further.

It may seem obvious, but if you choose to scatter ashes please consider the wind direction and location of yourself and other mourners. In times of stress we do not always think in a logical or clear way.

Some people may wish to have the ashes remain at home with them for the foreseeable future. If you wish to keep the ashes at home, please consider the implications of accidents or theft.

Certainly you should think about how long you would like to keep the ashes with you. After a few months you should carefully reassess what it is you are trying to do – eventually it is necessary to let go and create a new relationship, in memory, with the person who has died. Your keeping of the ashes may be denying this reality, and may also be denying others the ability to "visit" a person's final resting place.

If you choose to scatter or bury the ashes at home, consider that at sometime in the future you or your family may have to move house. It may be very significant for you that the new owners will then be the only ones able to easily access the site.

Look ahead to the Memorial section in Chapter 12 **'After the Funeral'** for further information and ideas in creating meaningful memorials.

Even if you do not move house, scattering or burying ashes at home may also mean that others cannot visit your memorial site easily.

Some people choose to scatter ashes at several significant places. Other people may feel that this is upsetting and inappropriate to consider.

If you wish to scatter the ashes then you need to consider that family and friends may wish to have a memorial plaque to visit, or at least a meaningful place where the ashes were scattered.

Please also take into account the possible desire of future generations to view a memorial to relatives past.

A visible memorial will often become even more meaningful and important as time passes, and there may be descendants yet to be born that will want to locate and spend time at a site dedicated to their long-ago ancestors.

In Summary – "The First Decisions"

You may answer yes or no, or provide details where appropriate

Burial or Cremation

Embalming

Viewing

Selection of Coffin or Casket

Memorials (This need not be decided now)

Chapter 5 Coming Together

It is universally acknowledged that some sort of organised gathering or even ritual is of vital importance when somebody dies.

> Coming together serves to address the reality of death, and often marks a primary point of reference through the journey of grief to recovery.

People have gathered together for many thousands of years to acknowledge the loss of loved ones. Even when death occurs in locations of isolation or extreme hardship, the human need to recognise and signify the passing of somebody cannot be underestimated.

Coming together strongly reinforces that those that are living are not alone. The comfort derived from the shared experience can be profound, extending not only into the weeks but also the years ahead.

If you are contemplating leaving instructions that your passing not be marked by a funeral, please think carefully. Your personal acceptance of "the way of things" may be denying others a fundamental need to "do something" in the face of such helplessness when a loved one dies.

You may feel that –

"It's a waste of time"

The funerals that you have been to in the past may not have been significantly personal, or individual, or relevant to either the person that died or those that gathered together to mourn that loss.

"Don't make a fuss of me"

When I'm gone I'm gone! Remember that the decision is not up to you if you have died, it's really up to those that are left. It may be your "selfless and humble" character that they need to mourn and celebrate!

Remember, a large part of the work of many grief counsellors often centres around ***helping people put the death of a loved one into a meaningful context.***

When someone's grief has become stuck and they are unable to move on, often recreating a meaningful memorial ritual will help.

A gathering together following a death is a *recognition* of a life that was lived, and is the first step to continuing on for those left behind. It reminds us that we are not alone and there are many others feeling the loss too.

It is the coming together that will remind us through the sometimes isolating loneliness of grief that we are not, and never will be, completely alone.

It can be difficult to make decisions about a meaningful funeral when a death is unexpected, or the person's wishes were not known.

You may need to consult with those people closest, and then please be assured that you will make the best decisions you can at the time.

There are many different words used to describe the events that people may gather for following the death of someone.

A general outline is as follows –

Viewing

A viewing is a time when people visit the deceased once they are placed in a coffin.

Viewings can be scheduled any time from minutes to days prior to a funeral. Sometimes they can be held between a certain period of the day (for example 1-3pm) and open to all who wish to attend, and then followed by a private funeral service.

At other times a viewing may form a central part of a funeral, with mourners invited to spend a few moments to bid farewell to the physical remains of the deceased.

Funeral

A funeral is a gathering, prior to committal, with the deceased present. This is traditionally held in a building, usually a church or other appropriate and respectful place.

Memorial Service

A memorial service is normally held when the deceased's body is not present.

The body may have been buried or cremated elsewhere, or not have been recovered from the sea or some inaccessible place, or not yet released by an investigating authority, or may have been donated to medical science.

In the case of a public figure a funeral service could be for the immediate family and a public memorial service held later to allow others to mourn the deceased.

A memorial service could also take place at the scattering or interment of ashes at an outdoor location.

Funeral Procession

A funeral procession is a movement of mourners and the deceased from one venue to another.

This often occurs following a funeral service at a Church or other building, when people will travel together in an unbroken line to a cemetery for burial.

In some countries car headlights are switched on as mourners show they are part of the procession.

It is not unusual for the funeral procession to form a very important and meaningful part of the day.

Many years ago the traditional funeral procession took place as the deceased left the family home, where the family had cared for them until arrangements for burial had been made.

Escorting the deceased on their final journey can be a powerful ritual.

Committal

Committal is the moment when a body is lowered into the ground, or cremated.

Interment

Interment is the placing of a body or ashes in a memorial vault or similar place.

Wake

A wake is the term used to describe a celebration or more informal gathering following the committal or interment of someone that has died.

A wake often involves refreshment and can be anything from a shared cup of tea at a person's home, to a large event with entertainment and a chance to joyfully share happy memories of the deceased.

Where Will We Meet?

Perhaps the first thing to consider is where a remembrance or funeral will take place. Sometimes the decision regarding where to have a final farewell is very clear and straightforward, at other times it is not.

It is possible to choose more than one venue, with a different style of gathering or even different people attending each one. It is a very personal choice and you should choose what feels right for your situation.

A general outline may be as follows –

Prior to Committal or Interment	Church Chapel or other Reception Room
At Committal or Interment	Crematorium Graveside
After Committal or Interment	Memorial Service at a Church or other venue Wake or informal gathering at a venue Scattering of ashes
In the weeks following memorials	Placing of headstones or other Special dates or anniversaries

The choice of venues has definite implications for the style of gathering and remembrance that people will share.

How many people are expected or would like to attend?

Will there be difficulties if the weather is unkind?

Many people will plan to organise more than one venue, to cater for the many different facets to a person's life and the passing of that life.

Who Will Attend?

The second major consideration in organising a funeral is deciding on the people that will attend.

Do you want to allow all those who want to attend to do so?

Or would you prefer to have an open invitation for only some, or even none, of the remembrance?

Do you know how to contact all those that would like to be present?

Will the people be able to attend immediately, or will there to be a delay while they travel?

If there are complicated circumstances regarding who might attend a funeral, please look ahead to Chapter 7 – "When Difficulties Arise".

Consider who is to lead the service. Even the most informal gathering will need to have a beginning, a middle and an end. Somebody will need to indicate these to the people present.

Your leader could be –
A Religious Leader
A Funeral Celebrant
A friend or family member

Some Examples of Your Choices

Once some initial decisions are made, the day as a whole needs to considered.

Step into the shoes of other people that may be attending. You should start to gain a clearer picture of what would be appreciated so that everyone can feel part of the day. Please remember you cannot please everybody!

Take a few moments to picture the gathering, from the following points of view –

- Your own
- The person that died
- Close friends and family
- Distant family and acquaintances

You cannot possibly satisfy all expectations, but it is worth a few minutes to imagine how you might make others feel welcome and included.

Here are just some examples of gatherings that you may feel are appropriate for your family –

- You may wish to have a service at a church, or many Funeral Directors may have a chapel or reception room available at their premises.

- You may wish to hold the service "in it's entirety" at a crematorium or have a burial service at a cemetery.

- A cremation may occur very quickly, followed by a memorial service days or if necessary even weeks afterwards.

- It is perfectly usual to have a service at a church or funeral director's premises and then to proceed to the cemetery or crematorium for a further final tribute at the time of committal. Sometimes it is appropriate for only close family to continue on, following a general invitation for all to attend the first service.

- For some families it might be preferable to have a larger, more public service either before or after committal. Sometimes a person can be so well known that many hundreds of people will want the opportunity to show their support and participate in remembering someone who has died.

- It is possible to have a viewing during or prior to a service. Sometimes it is not appropriate, and sometimes it is not wanted. Some religious or personal beliefs may dictate whether to have a viewing or not.

- It is also possible to organise a viewing directly before the service, so that only those who want to attend may also have their wishes respected.

- Following cremation or burial, many people choose to have a reception or wake to remember happier times, catch up with friends and family and generally honour the deceased in a more informal atmosphere.

This may be held at home, the home of a close friend or family member, at the Funeral Directors premises, at a local club or other venue. Usually this is a relatively short event, however every family and every funeral will be different.

Whatever you decide to do, once you have made a plan (usually in consultation with others) you need to stick to it.

The details will unfold in the coming days, but the possibilities for who, where and when are endless and you need to keep the framework of the day as clear and decisive as possible.

There will be opportunities to add details and incorporate other's suggestions as you go along, but the logistics of your planning must remain stable.

Bringing People Together

When people are informed of a death, the shock of the loss is followed by a desire to get together with others, to share their feelings, memories and initial responses.

Some may not wish to talk too much, others will talk and gather conversation with anybody that will listen, but all will feel the temporary isolation as we are reminded yet again that "everything that is born must die".

> Specifically, people need to know –
>
> ***where*** and ***when*** to meet
>
> any ***help*** they can offer with tasks
>
> ***how*** to show their support
> (for example, to visit or not visit you)

Sometimes there will be conflicting ideas in how best to honour and remember a loved one. You may wish to look ahead to Chapter 7 **'When Difficulties Arise'** if arrangements are not progressing smoothly.

Death does not exclude us from the problems of life, and our first emotional reactions in grief can place obstacles in the way of moving forward easily.

When you first let people know of the death, it is an advantage if you can also inform them as to how you will let them know the details of the gathering as they are decided.

Perhaps you or other close friends and family will telephone them.

Perhaps you will place a notice in the local newspaper.

There may be a clear network already existing through a club or workplace that can take over the role of letting some people know.

People will want to "do something" in response. Let them help you.

Their help could include –

- Letting others know of the arrangements
- Gathering photos or memories to share at the funeral or the wake
- Providing easy meals, or looking after the very young or the very old in your family. Simple tasks can sometimes feel overwhelming when grief is intense
- Coordinating company for you at home if you are uneasy about being left alone for long periods of time
- Appointing someone to answer telephone calls and be a reliable host in your home if you want to lie down for a few hours. Many people find great comfort in being present in a house full of guests, without actually being obliged to talk or interact
- Assisting you to write details down and keep track of the arrangements that are being made
- Helping you by looking after a specific task associated with the funeral, for example selecting flowers or finding a singer
- Organising the catering, or supplying specific food and drink for any informal gathering or wake
- Being patient, and just "being there" should you need them

Having others assist you in any way can make it much easier for you to rest, knowing that you are not neglecting your daily routine.

Reassure people that you will ask for their help if you need it, and then make sure you do!

Notice of Funeral and Other Considerations

When deciding on a day, consider whether everybody that needs to attend will be able to get there in time. This also applies to the time of day that is selected, for example an early morning funeral may not suit if many people have a three hour drive to attend.

Contacting relatives and friends in other countries can sometimes be difficult and time consuming, especially if different time-zones are involved. Be sure to enlist help where possible.

You may need to visit a place where the deceased attended or met others, in order to let people know.

A copy of the "Notice of Funeral" could be sent to a particular interest club or other group to ensure that everyone is notified.

Many people will keep any published notices regarding funerals or obituaries, so make sure you are happy with the wording.

"Notice of Funeral" in a newspaper may need to include the following details –

The basic format and location

- Where and when, including street address or special transport details, for all venues that will form part of the remembrance

- Whether certain parts of the funeral may be open to all, or if they are private gatherings and the "Notice of Funeral" is provided for information only

- If there is a special dress code, or other unique details

- Any requests for donations to specific charities in lieu of flowers

Identifying the person who has died

A short description can be very useful if the person that died had a wide circle of friends, or had moved area recently

Consider –

- Naming specific family or friends as principal mourners

- Listing the deceased person's address, or workplace, or other details that will clearly identify the person who has died

Other details may include

- The name of the Funeral Director so those who cannot attend may forward flowers or other communications
- Some people also like to include information on how the person died, or how the family and friends feel about their loss

Sometimes people use the Notice of Funeral to request donations to specific charities instead of bringing floral tributes to a funeral.

Other families may like to collect the flowers and pass them on to a particular hospital or organisation.

If you place a funeral notice in your newspaper or other methods of communication, do not be surprised if unexpected people arrive on the day.

> We cannot ever know the ways in which we touch other's lives, and the importance that they place on our contributions.
>
> It can be a humbling experience to realise that each one of us really does matter after all.

Similarly, do not expect a particular response from those that gather. We are all individuals, and the profound experience of grief can move us in unusual ways, or open old wounds of our personal losses and grief that we thought were buried and long-forgotten.

At a funeral, as people gather to remember a life lived, we are forced to reflect on our own mortality and the life we are currently living ourselves.

After a funeral some people and families will choose to place a "Thankyou" in a newspaper to publicly acknowledge those that attended or helped in other ways.

Some families and friends may also place "In Memorium" or "In Memory Of" notices on the anniversary of a death or other significant occasions such as birthdays.

In Summary – "Coming Together"

You may answer **yes** ***or*** **no*****, or provide details where appropriate***

	Where? What Time?	Who will be there? Who will lead us?	How we let them know
Before Funeral or Viewing			Eg Local newspaper
At a Funeral		Eg Minister Richard	
At Burial or Cremation	Eg Graveside, 2pm, Lawn Cemetery		
Social Gathering (Wake) or Memorial Service		Eg Uncle Peter	

Chapter 6 Completing the Arrangements

Now is the time to look through the next section of this book **'Inspiration and Integrity for a Meaningful Funeral'** and formulate your tribute.

Notice what seems relevant, or appeals to you and your family. You may also be inspired with your own ideas as you look through the suggestions given.

Leave this book on the coffee table, glance through it or discuss the ideas with a cup of tea and a few tears.

You will find that you will start to feel clearly about how you want to pay tribute to your loved one.

If you reject a particular idea outright, then you are closer to knowing exactly what it is that you do want.

A general outline of what to expect in a church, chapel and other services is given in the chapter "The Spoken Word".

You may find that you feel you are restricted by convention and ceremony in a organised religious service, or you may find great comfort in the tradition of a road well-travelled.

The enclosed 'When We Remember' CD contains many short musical excerpts. These have been specially arranged and professionally recorded to provide easy access to the creative minds of some great musical masters. Relax and have a listen through. You may be very surprised and inspired by where the music will take you.

> Once you have decided ***who, where*** and ***when*** it is very important to finalise ***what*** you will actually do there.

Once the primary decisions are underway, it is time to look at the specifics, and complete the necessary arrangements.

Some decisions will need to be made quickly as they will need a few days preparation. Other choices can be made a little later, as they need no preparation or presentation until the day arrives.

Early Decisions

Now that you have decided who will lead the gathering, meet with them and discuss what will take place when everybody comes together.

If you are going to be led by a religious leader, then you will be handing over the majority of the format and content to that particular religious convention. This is entirely acceptable, and can be of great comfort to follow in the footsteps of a time-honoured tradition.

There may still be some choices to make regarding sacred readings or music, and at the very least there should be reference to the character and life details of the person that died.

If the religious leader is to present the personal reference or eulogy, then they will need to be confident they can do this in an accurate and respectful way.

If you are able to, consider writing the eulogy yourself, either in full or in point form, so that you can be sure everything you would like to be said by the minister is said on the day.

Even if they knew the person that died very well, the religious leader will still need your input on the broader picture of their life. The picture you paint will be greatly enhanced if you are able to also invite input from other people who knew the person who died very well.

It is also important for you to confirm your expectations of what will happen, so that you are comfortable with the way the day will proceed.

If you are going to use a professional Funeral Celebrant or a friend or family member, then there will be many more decisions and expectations to be finalised. Take your time to thoroughly read through "The Spoken Word" and be sure to start as early as possible in creating a meaningful gathering.

Will there be funeral cars required to carry close friends and family, especially if there are two or more venues?

It is not unknown for cars and other forms of transport to form special roles in remembering the life of somebody, and you may feel that this is of special importance to you and your family.

While special consideration must be given to how to transport the coffin, many people also choose to travel together in a convoy between venues, for example from a Church to a Cemetery.

It can be appropriate to use the chauffeured cars of the Funeral Director, or you may prefer to organise other friends and family to drive particular people in their own cars.

When two or more venues are used, make clear to those attending if you would like them to travel between areas as you complete the funeral day.

Perhaps transport may need extra thought, if there is limited parking or an unusual venue. Ensure that the location can not be confused with another, especially if there are people attending from out of town.

You may need to provide a map, or a car pool meeting place, or coordinator for directions and lifts for elderly or non-driving mourners.

It may also be useful to include times for various venues, especially if a wake has been organised at a restaurant or other function place.

Will there be a written "Order of Service" given to mourners on arrival?

Sometimes it may be inappropriate or unnecessary, and at other times it could be a meaningful keepsake, especially for those who could not attend the funeral in person.

Digital scanning and imaging now makes it very possible and simple to include photographs in a printed Order of Service.

Although it may not be possible to finalise every last detail for a while, you must make contact reasonably quickly with the people that will do your printing. If it is a friend or family member, then you will still need to source the paper and organise how long it may take to complete.

The printers can confirm details such as the format you need to supply, costing on the various styles available, delivery options and of course their workload at a particular time.

It is to everyone's advantage to be aware of the completion time available.

Is the catering for the day underway?

People are very keen to help in any way possible, and looking after refreshments is one area that can be quite easily handed over to others.

Perhaps you need to confirm menu and price with an external supplier, or perhaps everybody that has offered to bring food and drink with them needs to know exactly what it is they are doing.

Particularly if you plan to have an informal gathering or wake at home, you should appoint somebody to oversee the organising. Details sometimes forgotten could include making sure somebody leaves early to be there to meet people as they arrive, or checking that there are enough glasses, plates or rubbish facilities.

Do the major participants know who they are and what they are doing?

It is no good asking somebody to sing on the morning of a funeral – they will almost certainly need time to prepare themselves not only physically but mentally.

They may need accompaniment or rehearsal, special equipment, or just space to rehearse in their mind the reality of performance at an emotional time.

The same goes for people that may be reading a poem or religious quotation, or perhaps writing a eulogy or other tribute. Do not underestimate the importance many people will place on what you have asked them to do, and also their intense desire to create the best tribute they can. All this at a time when our emotions can conspire to cloud our judgement and slow us down.

Are orders for extras such as flowers actually finalised, or did we simply discuss them?

This is one area where others can be very useful in confirming arrangements. While you and your close ones will be making decisions, it is not unusual to find that the final order has not been made.

It is a very sound idea to appoint somebody to be the overall "manager" for the many arrangements to be made. Many Funeral Directors will accept instructions on your behalf, and then pass on the invoices to you once the funeral is over.

Later Decisions

Do you want to display photographs or other items at the gathering?

Many people find this an easy and very personal way of honouring and remembering a life lived. Be sure to review the photos and items you have chosen, with a view to including as many important people and parts of a person's life as possible.

A display of this nature must be a balanced one, reflecting not only the person that died but also those who will attend. It can be a good idea to ask others to contribute.

Is it clear how people will arrive and leave?

It is worth reviewing your arrangements over time. You may suddenly realise that there are extra things to carry and now there is no room left in the car.

Or perhaps somebody needs to go elsewhere to collect things prior to the gathering and will be heading in the opposite direction for giving a promised ride to another person.

While many people will naturally fall in with what others are doing, it is worth thinking about your need for company versus privacy on the day of a funeral. You may wish to delegate a close friend or relative to keep an eye on how things are going and step in where necessary. Then again you may find that the gathering together of so many special people provides you with an energy that is most unexpected!

Are there any small gestures or words that you wish to include that will not involve a lot of preparation?

These could include things such as writing a short note to place inside a coffin, or pinning on a favourite decoration to a jacket you will wear on the day.

Perhaps you have to stop at a favourite spot to pick a flower, or even bring a photo of another deceased loved one with you to ensure that they can attend the funeral in spirit with you.

Sometimes a suggestion or chance remark from someone else suddenly seems a very appealing and worthwhile idea.

There are small but very meaningful things that can occur to you in the next few days. Write them down, or mention them to others to ensure you don't forget, or simply smile and let them go without action.

Do as much or as little as you please.

Do we wish to have a photographic or visual record of the day?

Some people would like a photographic or video recording of the day. This may be for their own needs, or to send to friends and relatives that were unable to attend.

If you would like a visual record of the day, be sure to consider exactly what you would like recorded. It may be an entire service, or simply a few informal photographs of mourners arriving and any floral tributes that are received. A professional will be sensitive to the sometimes invasive nature of using a camera, and if you ask a friend to take some shots it is wise to discuss how this will be achieved.

An example may be an agreement to only take photos from the side or behind, from a certain distance away, or not at all during certain parts of the funeral.

It is now possible to request video link in some larger city venues, to be transmitted at the time to people at great distances that could not attend.

The world wide comprehensive coverage with the internet now means that things only imagined as science fiction a generation ago are now a reality.

While often not high in quality, free internet programs such as Skype mean that with an inexpensive webcam it is possible for people to hear and see in real time the events at a funeral. Set up the camera behind the mourners, and the view will be as if you are sitting in the back row attending in person.

Do we wish to have a written record of those that attend the funeral?

The Funeral Director and their attending staff are very comfortable and experienced in establishing a condolence book for the day.

The book may be placed at the entrance of the venue on a stand or table, or names may be recorded in person by the Funeral Director as people arrive.

Should the Children Attend?

Now that you have developed a much clearer idea as to how the day will proceed, you are in a better position to answer this question.

For some families and cultural traditions there may be no question; of course the entire family will attend. Other traditions may require that no children attend, or even that only the adult men of a family or community are present.

Some families will decide that children will attend only parts of the day, perhaps because the formalities will be long or too mysterious for children to sit through.

Remember that children can be greatly influenced by their attitude and expectations of their parents. This will work both ways – it could either discourage or encourage them to be part of the day.

Younger children may be too young to remain quiet for long periods. This may be a distraction to other mourners, yet some have commented that this can be a good thing in reminding us that life does indeed carry on.

Children of all ages are surprisingly resilient and can often offer great comfort and insight when it is least expected. Generally if a child wants to attend or even participate in this very important family event, they should be allowed to do so. Their personal memories of the day can become very important as time goes on.

Be sure to consider carefully the words you choose when explaining to children what has occurred. It is most unhelpful to say that someone has gone to sleep and did not wake up; this and other euphemisms can be very frightening to children. Also consider that if you say that the person who died has "gone away", children may be tempted to try to find them or secretly believe they may one day return.

Perhaps call in the religious beliefs in your family, or even find an example in the animals and plants in nature to describe or reinforce what has happened.

Do not hide your own grief from your children. They need to know that it's ok to have powerful emotions, and to have good role models in how to deal with them.

Thankyou for Those Who Attend

You may wish to consider a gesture or small gift to say thankyou to those that attend.

Most often this is simply a matter of recording the names, and then sending a simple thankyou card for their attendance and condolences. Do not be pressured into organising these straight away – as long as you have some record of those who attended it may be weeks before these cards are sent. People will understand.

Sometimes it can be appropriate to consider a more active or immediate way to say thankyou. There are some traditional and modern options to consider –

Cycle of Life

Give a reminder of the cycle of life and the beauty of nature. Seeds before summer and bulbs after summer will provide a lasting display for the passing of a loved one in the weeks to come. You may find that certain flowers or plants are an obvious choice.

Charity Donations

If you have asked for donations to be made to a particular charity or organisation (for example a Cancer Research institute), you may find that the organisation receiving the donations may have thankyou cards or perhaps information brochures on how the donations will be used.

Rosemary

A sprig of rosemary is the traditional emblem of remembrance. Ancient Greek scholars would keep rosemary close by while they worked, or wear a sprig behind their ear during examinations. It was believed that rosemary increases our power to remember.

Order of Service

If you had an Order of Service for the funeral it will make a special keepsake for those who attended, and it could be sent to those that could not be there on the day.

Photographs

Photographs can easily be scanned and digitally reproduced on printed thankyou cards sent after the funeral. You have the advantage of less time pressure if you choose to do this after a funeral.

Poetry or Verse

As part of a written thankyou you may wish to include a special poem, verse or saying that was important to the person who died, or one that reflects the feelings of the family that remains.

Music CD

If the music used in a funeral or memorial was particularly appropriate or representative of the person that died, consider making up CDs of the music and passing them on to friends and family that attend.

Memorial DVD

If a collection of photos has been crafted into a short DVD to be played at the service, then you could also consider making multiple copies of this for the mourners.

Both of the previous ideas are particularly powerful if there are some mourners who are unable to attend through distance or illness. You could also consider an audio recording of part or all of the gathering – it would be a very strong and treasured token for those who were absent on the day.

Try to remember the other people that have helped you in the last few days. This could include medical staff, religious leaders or funeral celebrants, and any goods or services providers that may have been outstanding in their timely and professional delivery. A thankyou card after the event can mean so much.

There are many ways to say thankyou, and we all do so differently. Do not be concerned if you do none of these things. Everybody will understand that you are doing the best you can under very difficult and draining circumstances.

You may find that your good intentions do not go ahead because you simply do not have the energy to concentrate on getting anything other than the essentials done.

While you may wish to pass on your feelings of gratitude and thankfulness, now is not the time to particularly focus on the feelings of others.

> Every person that attends will have one clear wish for you –
> *that you cope with grief in your own way at your own time, and that you find peace as soon as you are able.*

In Summary

It can be a bewildering experience to confront the reality of death, even if the death was expected or we believe that we had prepared for it.

At a time of confusion and great emotion (and sometimes, through shock, a complete absence of emotion) we then try to organise a gathering together of people to remember the life that was lived.

There is a logical way forward, despite the burden and fog that grief often brings. Information and details will arrive, and then decisions will be made in turn, one step at a time.

It is always the job of the family to care for our own dead, whether through thought or action.

But we are not alone. We use the professionals – the Funeral Directors, health workers, religious leaders and so on – to offer advice where necessary. We then instruct these dedicated humanitarians to carry out our wishes.

Do not be tempted to trivialise or underestimate the importance of marking the death of a loved one. Refusing to acknowledge it will not make it go away. We need to find ways of integrating this enormous change into our future, in order to begin to slowly move on.

Acknowledge that a funeral is both a gathering and a separation.

> While we are farewelling one of our clan, we are also coming together to reinforce the love and common purpose that remains in our community.

It is a very important opportunity to gain support and perspective for the time ahead.

Involvement in the last earthly farewell to a loved one, whatever your beliefs, is always an important moment in our relationship – with both the person who has died and indeed with ourselves.

We shift our physical relationship into one of memory, when we choose to remember well those that we have shared life and love with.

Chapter 7 When Difficulties Arise

Sometimes things can be much more complex than we would like. For many reasons it can seem impossible to be able to find satisfactory solutions to difficult problems.

If this is your feeling, please do not think you are alone in your difficulty. Unfortunately death does not exclude us from the problems of life.

The task of organising a tribute, to honour the life of somebody who touched people in different ways, can be anything from a very straightforward to a very complex experience.

Many people will need to balance the needs and wishes of several members of a family. It can be very difficult to communicate effectively with people when they are separated by distance or circumstance.

Some people may rejoice in having shared time and love with somebody who has died. Others may be lost in sorrow, or other negative emotions such as guilt or regret.

What seems appropriate for some people may seem disrespectful to others.

The death of somebody close to us can bring to the surface many emotions, and some of these emotions may be entirely unexpected.

It is a time for those that are still living to come close and join in a common purpose. It is not a time to bring up old issues or past conflicts if it can at all be avoided.

Try to work together under the limits of grief, and the pressure of time.

The following pages provide examples of families that encountered difficulties when planning the funeral of a loved one. There are many reasons that you may be feeling emotionally strained if your grief is a complicated one.

Please do not be tempted to read this chapter merely for curiosity. You have enough challenges of your own at this time, whether real or imagined. Do not cloud and fill your mind with the problems of others.

If you are having a challenging time trying to organise a funeral, you may be relieved to know that families before you have been faced with difficulties and have found satisfactory ways to deal with them.

The solutions that you find to your problems will be as unique as the circumstances and difficulties themselves. Hopefully you may receive comfort and guidelines from the generously shared experiences in the following pages.

Who is the Chief Mourner?

For many families it is a relatively easy process to separate into clear roles and responsibilities when faced with the death of a loved one.

Someone will be the natural organiser, someone will take responsibility for caring emotionally for others, someone may be unable to help at all but will gratefully receive support from others, another person may be separated by distance but able to offer financial assistance at short notice, and so on.

There is no set requirement for *anybody* to do *anything*, however most times we just seem to be able to pull together and use our strengths to help each other through.

The death of someone often becomes a lot more complicated when they have married more than once, or have been step parents or step children.

Peter married in his twenties and had 3 children. Unfortunately by his mid-forties the marriage had disintegrated and they divorced. After a few years he met up with his second wife, and their marriage lasted another 14 years until Peter's sudden death at the age of 67.

Peter's adult children felt that they were best placed to make decisions about their father's funeral, and took charge of arrangements.

They were pleased to realise that in doing this a second dilemma was also solved – former wife and current wife could focus on their own personal loss, without ever coming into conflict, as both women had excellent relationships with Peter's children.

A Celebrant was organised to conduct the informal Christian-based service in a Funeral Director's reception room. He held two separate meetings in the days leading up to the service. The first was with Peter's children and their mother, the second was with Peter's second wife.

Both parties were comfortable that their knowledge of Peter through the various stages of his life would be well represented by the Celebrant, who was to give the main eulogy.

All seemed to be going well. On the day prior to the service, one of Peter's teenage grandchildren decided that he would collect some photos and form them into a short DVD presentation, with accompanying music, to play at the funeral.

He spoke with his father and 2 aunties, and they quickly rifled through their collections of photographs until they found 60 beautiful memories of Peter.

The photos stretched over 40 years, and Peter's adult children were genuinely pleased with the result. They felt that they had represented Peter well – his role as a father, sports enthusiast and keen community fundraiser through the decades were all clearly in the photos.

Unfortunately Peter's second wife was not clearly in the photos; in fact she was not in the picture at all.

When the time came in the service, the music and photos moved everyone to tears of laughter and sorrow. It really was an impressive and excellent tribute.

Little were people aware of the devastating effect that the lack of recognition in the photographic tribute had on Peter's second wife.

She was the current wife, the one with whom Peter had shared a bed with on the night he died and for the 14 years previous.

Unlike Peter's first wife she did not have the support of 3 adult children, and while she had graciously allowed Peter's children to take over the organisation of the funeral, now she was feeling very abandoned and almost deliberately excluded.

They had not thought to tell her about the powerful DVD that was to be such a centrepiece of the funeral, and they had not asked for her input with supplying a few photographs or perhaps a choice of song. She was unprepared and felt most unsupported, as if the love that she and Peter had shared for so long was not worthy of public recognition.

Of course this was not the intention of Peter's children. They had grown to love their step-mother even though she had not played a big part in their upbringing.

It was just that while looking through their own photos, Peter's children believed that the father they knew was represented well.

They looked at Peter through their own eyes, without considering the many roles that Peter had played in other people's lives as well.

Under less stressful circumstances the omission of Peter's second wife may have been easily forgiven, or perhaps not even noticed.

With a little more time to prepare, certainly Peter's children would have thought to mention the DVD to his second wife, asking for her share of photos to be included.

When somebody dies, our sense of place and self can be called into question, and at such an emotional and vulnerable time Peter's second wife was not able to keep perspective. She was very hurt by the perceived ignoring and rejection of the life she and Peter had shared.

Who constitutes the chief mourners? Does having a certain label entitle you to a greater or lesser right to grieve, or to be publicly acknowledged?

Step parents, step children, half siblings, gay partners, business or work colleagues, the great aunt that provided a home for you as you grew up, and so many other variations.

We cannot fit into neat categories all our relationships. We cannot explain sometimes the dynamics that enter our relationships as we continue on our way through the world.

- Focus on the person that has died, while providing space in the gathering to acknowledge all those that may have been important in their life. This may make some feel uncomfortable, but we all have right to grieve.

- Sometimes it is not necessary to mention or "label" those present at a service in priority order. Simply name the groupings of people present, and provide a silence space in the service to allow each person to remember what the person that died meant to them.

- Use a professional (Minister, Celebrant) or family friend to provide a central link between the mourners when necessary.

- Ensure that everyone is kept informed as decisions are made.

- It is generally not a good idea to allow the funeral to be very broken up and have sections allocated to various mourners. This will only work if somebody maintains overall control of the direction and flow of the remembrance.

- If in doubt, either leave it out or keep talking with the parties involved. At the very least, if a certain controversial element is eventually included, at least there will be no surprises for those present.

The Very Young

There will always seem to be something wrong with the natural order of things when a parent outlives a child. It can be very difficult to deal with the funeral arrangements of those we least expect to die.

There are many excellent resources now available for people that suffer miscarriage or the death of an infant. Our society is increasingly recognising the very real grief of parents whose dreams for the future, for both their child and themselves, have been shattered. Sometimes there will be siblings that will also be affected.

Ritual can play a very important role in publicly acknowledging the death that has occurred. When many mourners may have not met a young baby, or had a chance to share experiences, it can be difficult to find the words to describe the passing such a brief life.

> The loss of the very young can often be meaningfully acknowledged best not through words, but through action

Plant something. Write a poem. Visit a special place and hold a ritual. Scatter flowers. Float a bottle with a written message inside. Do something that marks your loss, something that defines a point in your journey through grief that you can look back on in the times to come.

Friends of a child who has died may benefit greatly from a viewing, or attending a funeral. It brings into the child's own reality the death that is being so talked of, and helps prepare a child for the absence of their friend in the times ahead.

Depending on the age of the child, activities can be organised to allow them to contribute to the ritual taking place.

If you hold a viewing, children accompanied by a loving and supportive parent can visit with homemade drawings or letters to place by the coffin. Some people have organised toys and art supplies to be available at the viewing, and have been amazed at the ease with which many children quickly include death into their experiences.

> My eight year old was quiet while we were there, and seemed instinctively comfortable with the respect needed for the occasion. We stayed 15 minutes, long enough for the parents to gather quietly while the children drew a picture for inclusion on a noticeboard at the funeral the next day. During the drive home, my child simply commented "He looked just like you said he would, and I'm glad they let him wear his black and yellow shoes. They were his favourite."

The death of a child is a complex loss of many things, for the family and friends that remain. Take your time, above all be gentle with yourself and do not hesitate to seek the help and support you may need.

Separation by Distance, Circumstance or Belief

Separation by Distance

Today we can be increasingly separated by physical distance from those we love. The modern ease of travel, and the far reaching networks of communication that now exist, have allowed us to easily accept jobs or take partners that are far away from the familiar places of our youth.

It is not until a crisis occurs that we realise how far away we really have travelled, and perhaps it is not so easy to drop our daily commitments to quickly be with our families.

There may be financial reasons, or perhaps we have children who cannot be cared for until we return. There are many reasons and responsibilities that may prevent us attending the funeral of one we love.

Do keep contact with family and friends that are at the location of the funeral in the days ahead, it is very important that you participate as fully as you are able in the decisions that are being made.

> Love knows no boundaries –
> ***You can still "be there."***

You may be able to take part in many ways, without interrupting the tasks that must be done on site. Delegate such things as –

- Choice of readings for the funeral (either from you personally, or to represent the family). Email and fax ensure that the written word travels very quickly.

- Preparing "thankyou cards" for those who attended (these will need to be posted anyway).

Participating through listening and talking, making small decisions yourself or being part of big ones, all these things will help prepare you for the day of the funeral.

Be sure to tell those around you what has happened, even if nobody in your current location personally knows the one who has died. Your friends will want to support you in your loss. Let them.

You may wish to perform some ritual or special arrangement at the time of the actual funeral. Be there in your thoughts, if not in reality.

Light a candle, read a poem out loud, get some people together to share your love and grief with, or go for a walk in nature to spend time alone with your precious memory.

Do something that is meaningful to you, whatever it may be.

Do not carry on as usual through the time of the funeral. Be part of the gathering by honouring and remembering, at the same time that others are.

Separation by Circumstance

Sometimes the circumstances of a death mean that there is no physical body present.

It may be irretrievable from the ocean or some other inaccessible place, it may have been donated to help others, or perhaps the physical remains of a loved one are simply not able to be part of a memorial service.

The actual committal of a body through burial or cremation, while a significant event, is still only a part of the journey of saying goodbye and assimilating a death into the continuing lives of those who remain.

The decision to go ahead with a meaningful tribute is a very logical and emotionally healthy choice to make.

You may well find that your own spiritual beliefs fully support the idea of a physical body being merely the "container" for somebody's spirit – and that your memory of that spirit can be cherished quite independently of the body.

If a family member has decided to donate their body to medical science, then holding a memorial is an excellent way of acknowledging the important and meaningful contribution that they have chosen to make for the benefit of our society.

Often if a body is to be donated to medical science then it will be removed very quickly – especially if potential donor organs are involved. This can be distressing if you are not prepared for this sudden absence of the physical presence of the deceased's body.

Having a meaningful tribute for a loved one, when their body is not able to be present, can be an excellent way of focussing on a life lived, not on the way they died.

Some families choose after a period of time to hold a memorial for somebody who has disappeared or gone missing. In many ways this remains valid even if the person returns – we all change and grow through experiences, and if these experiences are not shared then we may need to create a new relationship with the person when they return.

If the person does not return, then the families have created a meaningful point of reference in accepting the reality of the missing person.

> When somebody's remains cannot be present, it is through a memorial gathering that we can find the support and courage to bring death into the reality of our lives.

Separation by Belief

Many difficulties arise when mourners have very different beliefs from each other.

In our increasingly multicultural world, people are travelling and interacting more than ever. It follows that marriages, beliefs and cultural choices provide vast numbers of people who may come into conflict when it comes to how best to remember and respect the death of a loved one.

Tim's parents were devout Baptists, and raised their two boys accordingly, with the young family was very active in the church community.

While Tim's brother was accepting of his parent's beliefs and took them as his own, Tim struggled as a young adult to follow the family tradition.

Eventually Tim grew very separate from his family, and he found friendship and another way of seeing the world with the local motorbike group.

While not denying his parents their right to believe what they wanted, Tim now lived a completely different lifestyle.

Tim was very popular and well regarded by his group, and his skills in engineering and maintenance ensured that he had a very wide circle of friends. Tim's death at only 26 years old, in a road accident, was a terrible shock and loss.

Conflict in how to best remember Tim arose very quickly, as Tim's family and Tim's bike group informed each other of what they had planned for the funeral.

His family wanted a church service, with hymns, flowers and traditional Bible references.

The motorbike group told the family that they knew of Tim's views on religion, and that Tim had rejected outright the idea of God through a church.

The group insisted that Tim would be disrespected for the man he had become if the family went ahead.

Furthermore, they announced that none of them would attend such a funeral, leaving a very small gathering indeed to remember Tim.

The funeral according to the motorcyclists would involve everybody gathering on their motorbikes, informal story telling in memory of Tim, and a celebratory party for Tim involving alcohol and Tim's favourite loud rock music.

The conflict here was very clear, the two groups had fundamentally opposing beliefs. Tim's family had the legal right to determine what would happen to the body after he died, but they could not force the majority of the mourners to share their belief system.

Eventually the day went as follows –

Everybody gathered in the Baptist church and a traditional service was held to remember and honour Tim as a child, and of course most importantly as the son of his parents. Although mostly silent, the group attended respectfully.

Following the service, the group provided a very big motorbike guard of honour to escort Tim's coffin and the family on the way to committal.

Tim's family then attended the wake organised completely by the group. Tim's parents understood that their son had become a man and had a chosen to live a particular lifestyle.

Although they only stayed a short while, Tim's parents were made very welcome and they were pleased that they had attended.

You can see that the effect of the two parties coming together is very powerful. Each was able to see more clearly the role of the other in making Tim the man he had become. These revelations provide understanding and comfort for all concerned.

Everybody had been able to find a way to create a meaningful remembrance for a much loved young man.

If you find that there is conflict in what constitutes a meaningful farewell –

- Do everything in your power to reach a compromise, without compromising on your own integrity or beliefs. Respect that we are all different.

- Focus on the person who has died, while acknowledging the many ways that they communicated with people over the length of their life.

- Maintain strong communication between the parties, even if this needs to be through a third person.

- Even if agreement cannot be reached and certain disputed items do go ahead, then at very least you must ensure that everybody attending knows what will take place; that there are no surprises to distract from the important personal experiences on the day.

In another situation, a long-term mistress was phoned by the brother of the deceased man. The brother told her that while the mistress's name would not be mentioned at all in the funeral, the wife had acknowledged that the mistress had a need to attend.

In a brave and wise decision by the wife, she had retained control and primary status in the proceedings.

There would be no shock for her on the day – she knew that she may see the face of the mistress, but her generous act ensured that she would not be approached or challenged at a later date.

The wife would be able to focus on her grief and honestly acknowledge the passing of her husband, with all his faults and shortcomings.

> You do not have to compromise your beliefs – just compromise how you share the space with others when honouring a loved one.

Emotionally Challenging and Difficult Deaths

Perhaps you are in the unfortunate situation of facing a death complicated by intense conflict or negative emotion.

If you are to attend a funeral, and you expect other people to be there that you have not communicated with recently, or feel unable to share space with, you must keep focus on *why* you are there.

Your conflict will always be a two-way situation; even if you believe there is a "right" and a "wrong", both parties will be uncomfortable.

You should not expect or attempt reconciliation at funeral. Perhaps if there is a gathering or wake after the committal you may wish to acknowledge each other's presence, but emotions will probably be too strained in anticipation and grief prior to this.

You will be confronted with many emotions, some perhaps unexpected. Be sure to have a friend or partner to attend with you and provide personal support.

Remember that once words are spoken they can never be taken back; even an apology can not undo what has been said. Keep a wise counsel, respect everybody's need to attend and above all focus on the person who has died – this is the reason that you have all gathered on this particular day.

There will be plenty of time in the days and months following to consider your thoughts and emotions, and even renew communication.

If you are not invited or welcome by the principal mourners at a funeral, hold your own remembrance. See the ideas mentioned earlier in "Separation by Distance" to help you craft your own appropriate and meaningful farewell.

If person who died was disliked by you, take the opportunity to fully participate in the experience of the funeral. Time continues, and you may be able to reframe your present reality, or perhaps remind yourself of forgiveness in order to close a chapter.

Sometimes a death can occur in very difficult circumstances. Some deaths will challenge our very outlook and view on reality. If a loved one has met a particularly upsetting or distressing end to their life, there are certain things that may help –

- Focus on the life lived, not the way they died.
- Acknowledge that the few days between death and committal or remembrance ceremony should be considered a special and sacred time.
- If you feel anger, revenge, guilt or other difficult emotions, try to put them aside for now. Even if government authorities are involved, they will do their best to respect the family's right to privately mourn a loved one in the days following a death.

These intense times will become a little clearer and less overwhelming as you travel through the coming weeks and months.

Seek help and perspective from those around you, and do not hesitate to accept professional assistance from people trained to deal with situations most of us would find too challenging to contemplate. Rest assured there is always a way forward, no matter how impossible this may seem in the beginning.

Following is an example of when death tests our belief in spirituality, others and ourselves. You may find some comfort in the experiences and insight of the people involved.

Mary and her younger sister were greatly saddened when their mother died from a short illness with cancer. Barely teenagers, they managed to piece together their lives and continue on with their schooling and adolescence.

Their father was devastated, and he became increasingly lonely and withdrawn. The girls were quite relieved when he finally took another partner a few years later. They hoped the new marriage would be able to bring some happiness into their lives again.

Unfortunately the mental illness of their father did not improve. The tension became unbearable when the new baby was born. No longer was his new wife able to give him the attention that he had come to rely on, and Mary's father suffered a true psychotic episode.

Having lost all touch with reality, Mary's father became so enraged that he stabbed his wife, their baby, and then turned on himself.

The three bodies were found by a neighbour, and the attending medical staff and police discovered that only his wife had survived the terrible attack.

Mary's family were immigrants and had no relatives in the same country. Mary and her sister were cared for by neighbours in the following days, and slowly started to comprehend the unthinkable events that had taken place.

Mary had just finished school and her sister had another year to go. It was decided by the girls, and the social workers who were assisting them, that a funeral service would be very necessary to assist in bringing the deaths into reality.

As painful as it was, the girls were young adults and needed to feel as if they would be able to start to take control, to somehow find a sense of self to continue on with the rest of their lives.

They did not want to craft a long service, so mourners were asked to gather graveside for the burial of Mary's father and their baby sister.

On the day of the burial their step mother was also able to attend the burial, assisted by two nurses that accompanied her from the hospital. She was still terribly injured, with significant brain damage, but the doctors knew the importance of helping her to attend if at all possible.

It was not known at this early stage whether her memory of the attack may or may not return. If she did recover sufficiently, then her disturbing memory would need to be accompanied by the images of closure, the visual reinforcement that the attack could not continue or happen again.

It was such a terribly sad sight – two coffins, one so very small, attended by the two sisters, a small group of neighbours, some of the girls' friends and their parents, and of course Mary's wheelchair bound and heavily medicated step mother.

The minister leading the service was visibly shaken by the task ahead of him. He drew on spiritual and practical wisdom to create a meaningful gathering for those present.

He named the cause of death, and spoke of the pain that this would cause in the time ahead. He acknowledged by name the presence of the girls and their step mother.

He thanked the community for supporting the family and urged them to strengthen together in care of the girls.

He spoke of the way that our society can provide both togetherness and isolation; that it can provide enormous help but sometimes we need to ask for it ourselves.

He also spoke of the undeniable pain and confusion that must have existed in their father to commit such a terrible, unthinkable act. He urged those present to try to understand, and possibly in time to forgive.

If you are faced with taking some responsibility for a funeral in very difficult circumstances, consider –

- Try to put these deaths into context; to help those who are present start to find spiritual and worldly sense in what had taken place.

- Try to allow those present to remember the lives that had been lived, while not ignoring the way in which the lives had ended.

- Try to allow so many strong emotions to exist and be acknowledged in the funeral – rage, disbelief, guilt, anger, despair, compassion, regret, love.

- To re-affirm to those present the values of our community, the healing power of spiritual beliefs, and the extraordinary power of love and the human spirit.

In Summary

Sometimes the death of somebody can acutely highlight the problems that we can face as we make our way through the world. These problems can seem very difficult, or even insurmountable, when first considering your reactions to the death and planning a funeral.

Seek advice and perspective from those around you, and try to stay focussed on the event that has occurred, not the circumstances surrounding it.

Sometimes grief can be very complex and challenging. Try to remember that this is not always the case – death can touch us many times throughout our lives and each one will be unique and different from the one before.

Chapter 8 The Spoken Word

However personalised you wish the funeral to be, your selection of **venue** and **leader** will determine a great deal of the ceremony or ritual. Be sure that you have these two aspects arranged before you start further into the planning of what will happen there.

Even if you are sure that you will follow a clear religious tradition, it can help greatly to know what to expect on the day. Be sure to talk with your leader beforehand.

Introduction

There are many ways that we can choose to honour the death of a loved one, and there may be traditional guidelines to help us in creating a meaningful funeral.

- Religious Beliefs and Traditions

Many people will have a religious belief or tradition that they will choose to follow. There will be regional and other variations, but each traditional religious ceremony will have a core of ritual and rites that remain unchanged. Your religious leader will work with you to ensure that the appropriate action and words are used.

- Other Community Beliefs and Traditions

Sometimes we want to respect a certain belief, while also incorporating more individual aspects into a remembrance. Perhaps the person that died had a particular belief, and you have another. Speak with the religious leader that will conduct the ceremony. You may be able to find a suitable compromise, or you may have to use a more secular celebrant or venue to have your wishes met.

- Non-Traditional and Individual Beliefs

If you do not have a religious belief, then you will craft your own remembrance with the help of a secular celebrant or other person that you choose to lead the gathering. There are many universal needs when people are grieving, and there is a natural flow in events to consider when planning a gathering.

A Word on Traditional World Religions

You may or may not wish to read about what others do. However, death is of course universal, regardless of our beliefs. It may be of interest to you to gain an insight as to how others around the world, and through many centuries, have viewed death and life.

John T Catoir ("World Religions" Alba House, 2004) notes –

> "Though we are all different... there are some startling similarities. The most obvious one is a common belief in the Golden Rule. ***Do unto others as you would have them do unto you*** is perhaps the most familiar and most basic ethical principle of mankind."

Christianity

All things whatsoever you would that men should do to you, do you so to them: for this is the law and the prophets. (Matthew 7:12)

Buddhism

Hurt not others in ways that you yourself would find hurtful. (Udana-Vaarga 5:18)

Confucianism

Is there one maxim which ought to be acted upon throughout one's whole life? Surely it is the maxim of loving-kindness: Do not unto others what you would not have them do unto you. (Analects 15:23)

Hinduism

This is the sum of duty: do naught unto others which would cause you pain if done to you. (Mahabharata 5:1517)

Islam

No one of you is a believer until he desires for his brother that which he desire for himself. (Sunna)

Judaism

What is hateful to you, do not to your fellow men. That is the entire Law; all the rest is commentary. (Talmud, Shabbat 3id)

Taoism

Regard your neighbour's gain as your own gain, and your neighbour's loss as your own loss. (Tai Shang Kan Ying P'ien)

Zoroastrianism

That nature alone is good which refrains doing unto another whatsoever is not good for itself. (Dadisten-i-dinik, 94:5)

Whether we realise it or not, we all believe something. This belief could be a that nothing exists other than what we can see with our own eyes, or it could be a highly prescriptive way of living and being that is supported by ancient texts and evolved over centuries of culture, study and inspiration.

Of all our life experiences, birth, and especially death, can cause us to re-examine our belief systems with heartfelt passion. This can be a good thing – we will grow spiritually, emotionally and intellectually. We will either reject or re-confirm even more strongly our current beliefs.

There are essentially four perspectives that human culture has developed on our spirituality over many centuries. These are briefly summarised as follows –

The Atheistic World View –
"No God"

Atheists see man as supreme in the universe; he can master nature and solve all problems through science and technology. They see that we are all our own saviour, and that there is no intervention in our life except our own. Atheists can see that life is not pointless however; even after we die every word and deed will continue to have far-reaching consequences through the lives of those we touched while living.

The Monist World View –
"All Is One"

The clearest example is found in the Hindu religion, where it is believed that there is an all-pervading world-soul called "Brahman". The Law of Karma, which is the basis of the belief in reincarnation, states that everything which now exists came from Brahman and will eventually be absorbed back into Brahman. We lose our individual status from this life when we die; we are all ultimately part of the same one.

The Polytheistic World View –
"Many Gods"

Generally, polytheists live in awe of the spirit world. They may identify natural events with Devine beings (for example, a God of Thunder) or believe that every living creature has its own soul. Polytheists include worshippers of mythical gods, nature worshippers, many ancient or traditional indigenous cultures, and animists.

The Monotheistic World View –
"One God"

Judaism, Islam and Christianity all centre on the belief that man and nature were created by one supreme God. Jews and Muslims believe that there is an infinite chasm separating them from their creator, although God's complete authority can still be delivered on an individual basis. Christians agree with this, but also believe that God bridged the gap and came to live among us as Jesus Christ. These 3 religions make up the vast majority of current world religions, and are also referred to as Abrahamic religions as they all share a common linage through Abraham.

Some Examples of Religious Traditions

While there are generally considered to be only a handful of major world religions, there are of course great variations on how these are practised in our daily lives.

Differences in regional traditions and even personal observation of the sacred text allows for many styles of worship within the one religion.

Everything from fundamental to progressive interpretation of text, coupled with the more human characteristics of those who may lead a community in its interpretation, will have a bearing on the traditions of a particular religion.

Funeral rites may serve to reinforce a common faith, to mark the passage of a person from life to death, to secure the welfare of the dead, and to comfort the living.

There may be rituals attached to –

- Preparing for death
- Watching over the deceased person's body and preparing it for committal
- Gathering together to honour the deceased
- Committal of the body through either burial or cremation
- Observance of rituals for periods of time after the death

In all rituals or ceremonies where the body or coffin is present, the actual moment of departure is a particularly emotional time. This could be the lowering of a coffin, the closing of a curtain, or any other symbol to indicate the final departure of the physical presence of the person that has died.

Following are listed the major organised world religions and a very brief outline of death and remembrance practices.

Christian Traditions

Christians believe that God sent his son Jesus Christ to live among us, that He died for our sins and then rose from the dead. Through a relationship with Jesus Christ, people will be granted admission to Heaven for a life ever-lasting in the presence of God.

Christianity includes many Churches that we may think of as separate, but in fact they share a very common basis. Examples of Christian Churches include Anglican, Baptist, Catholic, Evangelical, Protestant and many other denominations.

While it is difficult to generalise, Christian traditions may include the following rites or rituals –

Burial is often preferred over cremation.

The body of the deceased is usually present at a funeral.

Candles, holy water and other items may hold significance during the funeral rites.

The Bible is quoted to provide continuity before and after death, reinforcing the teachings of Christianity.

A typical Christian service may include –

The Bidding

Mourners are welcomed, and asked to give thanks for the life of the deceased and grieve their loss.

The Word

This is the main part of many Christian funeral services. Literally, the Word refers to what the Bible and Church says about death. It can be expressed through prayers, hymns or readings from the bible. Many denominations are comfortable with appropriate secular poetry readings.

The Eulogy is also included here – a reflection by one or more speakers on the individual life of the deceased.

Prayer
Mourners are invited to remember their relationship to the deceased and review their own lives in relationship to God. There is usually reference to the death and resurrection of The Lord which expresses grief, sorrow for wrong-doing, remembrance, thanksgiving and the triumph over death.

The Commendation and Farewell
Special words to wish the soul of the deceased to find rest, peace and a life hereafter. It can also include an opportunity for the bereaved to say their last goodbyes.

The Committal
When the coffin is lowered into the earth for burial or move behind a screen at the crematorium.

Within each denomination often exists many styles of worship and corresponding funeral traditions.

There is great variety in what is considered acceptable in music and text, from the use of sacred through to secular sources.

Islamic Traditions

Muslims believe that death is a departure from the life of this world, but not the end of a person's existence. Eternal life is to come, and prayers are offered for God's mercy so that the departed find peace and happiness.

While it is difficult to generalise, Muslim traditions may include the following rites or rituals –

Great care and respect is taken as the family and community members wash and shroud the body.

The body of the deceased is usually buried as quickly as possible.

Funeral prayers (salat-l-janazah) are offered outdoors in a courtyard or similar place, not inside the mosque.

While all members of the community attend funeral prayers, only the men accompany the body to the gravesite.

The body is buried on the right side, facing Mecca.

The Qur'an is quoted to provide continuity before and after death, reinforcing the teachings of Islam.

A 3-day mourning period is observed, with widows mourning for an extended 4 months and 10 days (Qur'an 2:234)

Hindu Traditions

A belief in the cyclical reincarnation of the soul is a foundation of the Hindu religion.

While the ultimate goal is to transcend the need to return to life on earth, Hindus believe they will be reborn into a future that is based primarily on their past thoughts and actions.

Cremation is a ritual designed to do much more than dispose of a soul's bodily remains; it also releases the soul from its earthly existence.

While it is difficult to generalise, Hindu traditions may include the following rites or rituals –

A cremation ceremony begins with the ritual cleansing, dressing and adorning of the body by all members of the family.

Prayers are chanted to invoke the aid of Yama, as the body is transported to the cremation site. Traditionally it is usually only the men that attend.

The chief mourner, usually the eldest son, lights the funeral pyre. For a modern urban funeral the chief mourner will use the controls at a crematorium to start the process.

To ensure the safe passage of the soul following its release from the body, an 11-day ritual (shraddha) is observed. Many also observe 31 day and yearly memorials.

It can be considered important to scatter ashes upon the sacred river Ganges.

Buddhist Traditions

Buddhism is practiced in many forms throughout Tibet, China, South-east Asia, Japan, and world-wide.

While it is difficult to generalise, Buddhist traditions may include the following rites or rituals –

Cremation is preferred quite soon after death, although sometime a prominent member of society may be delayed up to a year afterwards, in order to show respect.

Many Buddhists believe that between death and rebirth there is an intermediate period, known as Antarabhava in Sanskrit or Bardo in Tibetan. It is an important time and may have an influence on the form that the rebirth may take.

Viewing the deceased body is encouraged, often forming a central part of the ritual.

Monks may offer prayers, and they will be returned with food and drink from the female members of the family.

The period of prayers and then care of the soul could be anything from 3 days up to 100 days.

Wealthy families may sometimes offer at the cremation books and other written material containing Buddhist teachings. These represent a tribute for a commendable life of service and also reinforce the Buddhist faith.

Jewish Traditions

All Jewish traditions regarding death are for one of two reasons: respect for the dead (kvod hamet) or to console those left behind (nihum avelim).

A vigil is kept constantly over a person's body from the moment of death until burial. "Shiva" is a 7-day mourning period that begins immediately after the funeral and is based on the Hebrew word for seven – a mystical number in many traditional religions and also the number of days that God took to create the world.

Candles may be lit, mirrors may be covered in the chief house of mourning, and visitors are welcomed throughout this time in order to care for the immediate family. The principal mourners are encouraged to do nothing other than stay at home, remember their grief and be emotionally present at this special time.

While it is difficult to generalise, Jewish traditions may include the following rites or rituals –

Once a deceased person's body has been washed and prepared according to tradition, the coffin is immediately sealed and no viewing is permitted.

Most Jewish funerals are held at a Funeral Home, with a synagogue funeral usually reserved for a person that was particularly prominent in the Jewish community.

It is common to have several people deliver a eulogy (hesped) at the start of the funeral.

The funeral and burial will usually take place on the same day as the death, or if not possible, the next day.

The Torah is quoted and certain ritual prayers are offered to provide continuity before and after death, reinforcing the teachings of Judaism.

Some Examples of Other Beliefs and Community Traditions

There are some beliefs that do not have a central text as the source of guidance or inspiration, but their philosophy or unity of purpose provides a very clear theme for our lives.

Our communities are made up of many organisations that unify us, and these organisations or beliefs may have significant impact in reflecting on a remembrance for a life that was lived.

There are many traditions and beliefs that may form the basis of a remembrance for somebody. Many countries and cultures will have regional variations or traditions that can be very meaningful, especially if a family is no longer living in that country.

Following are listed just some examples of the way that our purpose and life can be reflected in a funeral. Some of these tributes can often be incorporated into either a traditional religious or non-traditional funeral.

Community Organisations

When a person has devoted considerable time and energy to a particular cause or service, then that organisation may wish to honour their death with a ritual or specific tribute. Every community has many such organisations. A few examples include the police, fire and ambulance services, or non-career based organisations such as the Masonic society.

Men and women that have served their country through the armed services are often offered certain rituals at the time of a funeral. Australia has a very strong funeral ritual for ex-Armed Services personnel, through the RSL (Returned Services League). Many other countries will have similar traditions.

Armed Forces traditions could include –

Several uniformed personnel present to act as a guard of honour.

The use of certain phrases and other rites in the funeral service.

Playing particular music normally reserved for active life in the armed service.

Humanist

(also known by other names)
Sometimes a belief may be in the absence of God or other figure, and instead focus on the natural world as a source of wonder.

The guidelines for how to conduct our lives can be drawn from logic, and an understanding that all of our actions have the potential to impact on all other life forms on our planet.

Many people are growing in concern for the state and health of our planet's environment, and there are ways to incorporate this concern in a funeral.

Consider –

- Having a memorial gathering at an outdoor location of natural beauty or significance
- Sourcing a renewable resource or easily biodegradable coffin
- In memory of the person that has died, asking mourners to consider donating to focus groups that support environmental concerns
- Opting for a "woodland" or other "green" burial site. At these sites, instead of a large man-made marker, a tree or other feature is planted at the site of burial

Some Examples of Non-Traditional Services

Sometimes an individual may have not followed a particular religion, or given a priority to any other organisation or cultural tradition in their life.

A secular (or non-religious) funeral can still satisfy some powerful needs we all have at a time of death and grief, including –

- To connect with others, to support and encourage
- To remember and honour the person that has died

If there is no particular spiritual or other belief that forms a central part of someone's life, then it is through an individual's personal characteristics and interests that we can choose best to remember and honour them.

- To begin to find the courage to adapt to change and reshape our future
- To move our relationship with the deceased to one of memory
- To bring the reality of death into our present lives, providing a signpost along the journey of grief

Flowers for Frank

Frank was a landscape gardener and there was not much he didn't know about plants. He had disliked most of his limited school education, but his knowledge of Latin names, growing habits, plant care and design was stunning and he constantly amazed people with his encyclopaedic knowledge.

When Frank died mourners were asked to bring a small bunch of flowers as they arrived at the outdoor funeral, and these were all placed together in several baskets. The flowers and plants displayed were a clearly visible reminder of Frank, and the beauty he found in the natural world.

At the conclusion of the funeral, each mourner was asked to take home with them a different bunch of flowers to one they arrived with. It was a powerful symbol of the beauty of growth and shared natural resources, of Frank and his life's passion, and of community spirit and connectedness in remembrance of Frank.

During the eulogy delivered by his brother, many of Frank's characteristics were given Latin names or compared to the growing habits of certain plants, much to the delight of all present.

The Celebrant leading the remembrance mentioned God as the creator of all things, as well as the wonder of nature as the evolutionary source of the stunning beauty of the environment all around us. He also mentioned that Frank was now at peace "however you believe that to be", providing space for religious and non-religious mourners to share comfort together – irrespective of their individual beliefs.

Everyone present found inspiration in remembering and honouring Frank's dedication to caring for that which he loved best. The lesson extended to include caring for everyone present, and a great sense of togetherness and mutual support extended throughout Frank's family, friends and workmates.

It seemed most appropriate that Frank was buried in an environmentally-friendly coffin, with a small stone carving and a magnificent young tree planted in his memory.

Another Social Gathering for Catherine

Catherine was only 17 when she died suddenly in a car accident. The shock of such an unexpected death was immense throughout her many young friends. Catherine's older relatives were devastated, but it was the teenagers that really needed to do something concrete to bring her death into their limited life experience.

Catherine's family asked everyone bring a favourite photo with them to the funeral, to be placed on a board. Small captions were added on purple paper provided on the day (Catherine's favourite colour) and the boards provided an excellent focus for Catherine's many friends to gather around, lovingly organising the display, as they waited for the funeral to commence.

The Celebrant welcomed everybody, and spoke of "all that is born must die" – strong words but true. She talked of the shock, the disbelief and the pain, yet also reminded mourners of the gift of life, and the great joy Catherine had brought in her short time with them.

Young mourners were invited to recall a story from school or social events, of which there were many. One by one, or in small groups, the teenagers came out to the boards and shared their memories of the photo they had brought and what Catherine had meant to them. They cried, they laughed, and they also showed instinctive insight and maturity.

Two of Catherine's favourite songs were played, and her trademark purple coat was draped over the coffin.

Family were given great comfort from the input of her many friends and the vital, loving role she had played in so many people's lives. The teenagers had been encouraged to participate, and in doing so they could start to make sense of what had happened and bring Catherine's death into reality.

At the end of the funeral, all of the teenagers declined to take back their own photos. Some left them with the family, and others swapped them with friends to ensure that Catherine's memory would not be forgotten.

Crafting a Eulogy

Eulogies are the words that are spoken during a gathering that refer specifically to the character and life of the person who has died.

Every remembrance will at least mention the name of the person that has died, and the most powerful funerals are often those that can use a eulogy to truly recreate the presence and legacy of the individual that lived among us.

It is impossible to find and speak all of the words we need in order to recreate who somebody was and what they meant to us. We all relate on different levels, at different times of the day or year, sharing different relationships and experiences.

Some families will have a natural choice of person to deliver a eulogy. Perhaps there are a work place or favourite leisure club that would also like to speak.

In many religious traditions the leader of the service will give the main eulogy and then invite others to step forward for a short time. In some traditions there may be no mention of the individual, this would occur at another time at less formal gatherings.

Most people consider it a great honour to be asked to deliver a eulogy.

Who does the Eulogy?

The religious leader or celebrant

Even if the leader of the funeral knew the deceased well, they certainly were not present for all of the aspects of someone's life. Celebrants or ministers will very often spend an hour or two gathering information during a meeting with friends and family in order to craft a personal and accurate eulogy.

A close friend or family member

There may be an obvious family member or close friend that knew the deceased very well and is comfortable with public speaking. It is usual that they will also consult with others, informally, to ensure that they can represent the many relationships that exist in our lives.

Several people may be asked to give short recollections

If a person had a busy life, then there may be several aspects that should be mentioned. Sometimes we need several people to do this.

If two or more speakers are to be asked, then give clear direction as to how long they should speak for. Let each speaker know who else will be speaking, and ensure that everybody is aware of their role in helping to deliver the eulogy.

Sometimes a eulogy is opened to include anybody who may wish to speak at the actual time of the funeral

This can be a wonderfully powerful way of remembering somebody at a funeral, however there is also the possibility that an "open floor" can not work as well as planned. Many people would prefer to know in advance that an open invitation to speak will occur, in order to prepare something meaningful and well-crafted.

If you are to open the eulogy to all who wish to participate, then the leader of the gathering should consider –

- Clearly state the length of time mourners should speak for. For example –

"We now invite anybody that wishes to speak further in remembrance of (the person that died). Please come forward freely, and focus on one aspect of your relationship with him/her. A few short words will allow all who are present the opportunity to participate."

- The leader of the gathering must be prepared and willing to step in if somebody is speaking for too long, or is unable to remain focussed on what they are saying.

How do I Prepare a Eulogy?

With any public speaking preparation, there are several logical stages to work through. Be sure to set aside enough time, and work out exactly how long you will be able to spend on each stage before the day of the funeral.

Planning

Prose

Practice

Be positive, have courage, and trust that you know what to say. It does not have to be perfect, very few of our relationships and communications ever are.

In being asked to deliver a eulogy you have been offered the trust of the close friends and family, and as long as you write from the heart your eulogy will be gratefully accepted by everyone present.

You may even find it an easier and more joyful task that you had expected.

The first thing to do is work out a timetable, considering –

- The number of days you have to prepare and

- What hours in those days you will be able to devote to crafting a eulogy.

Do not be too concerned if in the end you were not able to follow this timetable.

You may find an hour or two is enough time, or you may find yourself being led in different directions and preparing the eulogy takes much longer than expected.

Adjust your timetable accordingly, and continue to follow the 3 steps in order.

Planning

(Deciding what to say)

Your preparation may have started some time ago if a death was expected, or perhaps you are in shock at a sudden death and will not have the luxury of time. Even if you are not directly representing others, it is always a good idea to talk through your plans.

As you start to consider what you might say, be sure to write down your thoughts.

Do not be concerned with how perfect they are, or in what order they might come. Be comfortable with leaving things for a while, and returning at a later time.

Remember you are trying to capture a person's experiences, contributions and character. Too often a eulogy is reduced to a collection of dates, without evoking many memories of the day to day life that was lived.

Perhaps it will work well to consider the person in the many roles they may have played in our lives – for example as a daughter, wife, mother, secretary and friend.

Sometimes a chronological order will work well if there is a common theme – for example frequent travel, a love of the familiar, or always helping others.

Often a eulogy will work just as well if focus is given to only a small part of their years, especially if they have had a very full life.

Perhaps there will be several speakers and you have been asked to focus only on one particular aspect of their life, or you may just feel that you only want to touch on certain areas that are relevant to you and your shared experiences with the deceased.

Perhaps a full life will mean there are many things that those present did not know. It can be very powerful to briefly talk of each decade lived, with reference to the highlights and challenges. Earlier experiences may not have talked about often, or have been powerful in helping to shape the person they became.

It can often be the case that we are pleasantly surprised and feel we know someone even better when we listen to others describe their relationship and experiences in detail.

There are several questions that can help generally in deciding what to say –

- What are the things that they will be remembered most for?

- What were they most proud of? What hopes and regrets did they share with you? What annoyed them? What excited them? What was important to them?

- What words, actions, thoughts, situations, philosophies, times of day, foods, places and activities may remind you of them most?

- How do you think they would like to be remembered? What characteristics or actions will live on through the lives of others?

Sometimes there is a short story that can be an excellent way of highlighting many of these aspects together.
A retelling of a camping trip could highlight a passion for fishing, the importance of friendship, a desire to enjoy life one day at a time, a dislike of being tied down to work commitments, a remembrance of happy family childhood memories, a great sense of humour and a lack of cooking skills!

You may wish to include a little of what you will personally miss about them, and what they have taught or meant to you.

Sometimes it is appropriate to speak a final public conversation, acknowledging some of what remains unsaid when somebody dies. Be sure to respect others present when you consider your personal words.

Perhaps there is something that you have learnt through the example of their life, or their death, that is particularly important to share.

Sometimes quoting a particular saying or favourite short poem of theirs can be particularly meaningful.

It can be wonderful to use some of their own words if the person was a writer, and there may be other things to draw on if the person was creative or enjoyed the arts.

Prose

(Selecting the words to use)

Once you have decided on a collection of thoughts, or settled on a theme, or gathered all the information you need from others, it is then time to write.

You should aim to have a well written and easily read copy of the eulogy at least the day before the funeral.

Your will need time to practice and be comfortable with delivering a eulogy, and although many thoughts will continue to arise as to what might be said, resist the temptation to keep adding words and ideas. We can never say or include everything we want to.

It is a very good idea to write down word for word what you want to say, as it is entirely appropriate for the celebrant, minister or another family member to step in and read for you if you are unable to continue on the day.

If you are not comfortable with public speaking, or feel you may be very emotional on the day, then do take the time to write well.

Professional writers will notate many drafts before they are satisfied with the final version.

Some simple things to consider include –

- Are there any often repeated words? (for example very, I, he, and)

- Are the sentences too long? (It is much easier to read short sentences well)

- Do many sentences start the same way? (for example he, then, when)

The final version of your eulogy will be confirmed once you have started the next and final step – reading the eulogy out loud.

Practice

(How to deliver the words)

It is very important that you read out loud your written words. You do not need to do this to an audience, although if you are very nervous it will definitely help to have one or two people to practice on and reassure you before the actual day.

Reading out loud will make very clear to you any problems with your writing style, not picked up in the "Prose" section of your preparation. You can also time your spoken eulogy, and perhaps reduce some of what you were planning to say.

You will instantly discover sentences that are difficult to read, any unnatural pauses or awkward combination of words, and many other details.

Do not be afraid to re-write a section or two. It will often mean simplifying, not adding to, what you have written.

Although you should have a copy of exactly what you want to say, you may be comfortable simply using your words as a guideline. Highlight in colour the major points or phrases, and refer to your notes as you need to.

Hints for delivering a Eulogy

- The unusual and highly emotive setting of your talk may bring unexpected feelings of nervousness, even if you are used to public speaking.
- All performers get nervous, always. The difference with a seasoned performer is that they are used to the unusual physical and emotional feelings that come with being nervous, and expect them to occur. Without the surprise of the unusual feelings, they are able to remain clear and continue as normal.
- Speak slowly, speak quite loudly, and breathe! It would be a shame for others to miss out on your lovingly thoughtful tribute. A smile will help enormously.
- If you find that you are unable to continue, try to see this reaction as an emotional tribute in itself.
- A simple glance to the leader of the gathering may be enough to steady you. Perhaps you can ask them to stand by your side, or even continue reading on your behalf while you remain with them.
- It is important that everyone present is able to understand your well-chosen words, and it is surprisingly common that we end up needing others to complete this for us on the day.
- Try to use high and low pitch, and don't be afraid to pause for a time. It allows others an important moment to reflect on what you are saying.
- If you are nervous, it is because it is important to you to do a good job. Remember everyone is wishing you well. Relax. Take your time.

Chapter 9 The Written Word

It is usually at times of great joy or pain that we may find ourselves "lost for words".

Perhaps there are no single words to express our emotions, but usually a carefully chosen group of words can come close to conveying our thoughts and feelings. Groups of words start to convey concepts, emotions and other more complex ideas.

We may be bursting with wanting to say something, but we just don't know how to do it. While we may struggle to find our own words, we are still able to recognise what we would like to say, when we read it from the pen of others.

We never walk alone, and sometimes it is much easier and more comforting to take shelter in the great wordsmiths and traditions that have travelled this road before us.

Following are some selections from centuries of sacred and secular (non-religious) writers. Some are entire poems, some are excerpts from poems or novels, and some are from sacred texts or Divine inspiration.

Perhaps you are looking for a reading to focus on the person that has died, or perhaps you prefer to find a reading that expresses your grief that they have gone.

It can be very memorable to consider writing your own funeral poems or tribute to someone that has died. "My One True Thing" by Lyn Anderson is an excellent example of poetry describing the characteristics or cherished memories of a loved one. It does not have to rhyme, and writing in short groups of words can condense our feelings into a very powerful tribute.

Children need to express their feelings too, and can often be a surprising inspiration with their intuitive ability to say clearly what really matters most.

As you look through the following pages, you should find that you are drawn to certain readings and not to others. There is no right or wrong in your selection. Hopefully you will find some comfort in the words and experiences of others.

I Am Not Alone

Claribel Alegria 1924 –
Nicaraguan Poet, translated by Carolyn Forché

I am not alone
and never will be

Your absence is my company

Farewell

Anne Bronte 1820 – 1849
English Poet, from family of literary women

Farewell to Thee! But not farewell
To all my fondest thoughts of Thee;

Within my heart they still shall dwell
And they shall cheer and comfort me.

Life seems more sweet that Thou didst live
And men more true that Thou wert one;

Nothing is lost that Thou didst give,
Nothing destroyed that Thou hast done.

Miss Me, But Let Me Go

Unknown

When I come to the end of the road
And the sun has set for me,

I want no rites in a gloom-filled room
Why cry for a soul set free?

Miss me a little – but not too long
And not with your head bowed low.

Remember the love that once was shared
Miss me, but let me go.

For this is a journey we all must take
And each must go alone.

It's all part of the master's plan,
A step on the road to home.

When you are lonely and sick of heart,
Go to the friends we know.

Bear your sorrow in good deeds.
Miss me, but let me go.

A Song of Living

Amelia Josephine Burr 1878 - 1968
American Poet

Because I have loved life,
I shall have no sorrow to die.

I have sent up my gladness on wings, to be lost in the blue of the sky.

I have run and leaped with the rain,
I have taken the wind to my breast.

My cheek like a drowsy child to the face of the earth I have pressed.

Because I have loved life, I shall have no sorrow to die.

I have kissed young Love on the lips,
I have heard his song to the end.

I have struck my hand like a seal in the loyal hand of a friend.

I have known the peace of heaven,
the comfort of work done well.

I have longed for death in the darkness and risen alive out of hell.

Because I have loved life, I shall have no sorrow to die

Footprints

Unknown

One night a man had a dream.

He dreamed he was walking along the beach with the Lord.
Across the sky flashed scenes from his life.

When the last scene had played,
he looked back at the footprints in the sand.
He noticed that many times along the path of life
there were only one set of footprints.

He also noticed that it happened at the very lowest
and saddest times in his life.
This really bothered him and he questioned the Lord about it.

"Lord, you said that once I decided to follow you,
you'd walk with me all the way.
But I have noticed that during the most troublesome times in my life,
there is only one set of footprints.
I don't understand why when I needed you most you would leave me."

The Lord replied,
"My son, My precious child,
I love you and would never leave you.
During your times of trial and suffering,
When you see only one set of footprints,
it was then that
I carried you."

Epitaph on William Muir

Robert Burns 1759 – 1796
Scottish Poet

An honest man here lies at rest,
As e'er God with His image blest:

The friend of man, the friend of truth,
The friend of age, the guide of youth:

Few hearts like his – with virtue warm'd,
Few heads with knowledge so inform'd:

If there's another world, he lives in bliss;
If there is none, he made the best of this.

From a Gravestone in Sutcombe, Devon

The lovely bud, so young, so fair
Called off by earthly doom,
Just came to show how sweet a flower
In paradise could bloom

My One True Thing

Lyn Anderson 1945 -
Australian Poet

My one true thing
I woke, you'd gone
Chance to speak
Gone forever

Plans to share memories of Home
Memories of abundance in hard times
Overflowing garden
Wild daisies flowing with the wind

Deep perfumed dark roses, stocks and carnations
Forever flowering succulents long before the fashion
Ripe mulberry, orange, lemons, peach and fig trees
Jam making sealed with hot glue

Constant warmth from a wood stove
Smell of a roast in the oven
Bread and butter pudding, the best I'll ever taste
Fruit salad and cream

Singing old fashioned songs
With old fashioned meanings
I could write a sonnet about your Easter bonnet...
You always hurt the one you love...

Lazy nights on a cool lawn
Millions of stars in a warm black sky
Talking of Robert Askin's politics
Dreaming of the best holiday and fishing spots on the coast

White sheets flapping with the wind
Stiff white tablecloths, folded napkins
Polished silverware
Flowers everywhere

Busy people, your home, my memories
My beautiful mother who never asked much from life
Yet gave so much to so many people
My one true friend, my centre, you're gone

Thank you for a gentle life with honest people
You warned me many times, I had no courage to see
You would say that's ok
But I want to talk to you today

I travel another road, one day at a time
Your memory my guide
You're with Dad, Thelma, Clem, Nana, Granddad and Jim
It's the way of things

Nourished by your generous gardens
Pouring onto pathways, climbing the cracks
Your generous kitchen nourishing all
I have one who is starving

I know you would help me if you could
But rest well my mother
Your work is done
I will carry on

Traditional Gaelic Blessing

May the road rise up to meet you.
May the wind be always at your back.

May the sun shine warm upon your face;
the rains fall soft upon your fields

And until we meet again,
may God hold you in the palm of His hand.

Eternity

William Blake 1757 – 1827
English Artist, Engraver, Mystic and Poet

He who binds to himself a joy
Does the winged life destroy;

But he who kisses the joy as it flies
Lives in eternity's sun rise.

The Hands of Time

Unknown

The clock of life is wound but once
No-one has the power

to tell just when the hands may stop
The year, the day, the hour

When you plan a kindly deed
Act now, use all your skill

The present only is our own.
Live, love, toil with a will.

Wait not until tomorrow
The hands may then be still

Remember

Christina Rossetti 1830 – 1894
English Poet

Remember me when I am gone away,
Gone far away into the silent land;

When you can no more hold me by the hand,
Nor I half turn to go, yet turning stay.

Remember me when no more day by day
You tell me of our future that you planned

Only remember me; you understand
It will be late to counsel then or pray

Yet if you should forget me for a while
And afterwards remember, do not grieve:

For if the darkness and corruption leave
A vestige of the thoughts that once I had,

Better by far you should forget and smile
Than that you should remember and be sad.

Poem

James Langston Hughes 1902 – 1967
American Author, Playwright and Poet

I loved my friend.
He went away from me.
There's nothing more to say.

The poem ends, Soft as it began –
I loved my friend

Even Such is Time

Sir Walter Raleigh 1552 – 1618
English Navigator, Historian and Poet

Even such is time, which takes in trust
Our youth, our joys, and all we have,
And pays us but with age and dust;

Who, in the dark and silent grave,
When we have wandered all our ways,
Shuts up the story of our days,

And from which earth and grave and dust,
The Lord shall rise me up, I trust.

Crossing the Bar

Lord Alfred Tennyson 1809 – 1892
English Royal Poet Laureate for 40 years

Sunset and evening star,
And one clear call for me!
And may there be no moaning of the bar,
When I put out to sea,

But such a tide as moving seems asleep,
Too full for sound and foam,
When that which drew from out the boundless deep
Turns again home.

Twilight and evening bell,
And after that the dark!
And may there be no sadness of farewell,
When I embark;

For tho' from out our bourne of Time and Place
The flood may bear me far,
I hope to see my Pilot face to face
When I have crost the bar.

So What is Love?

Unknown

So what is love? If thou wouldst know
The heart alone can tell:

Two minds with but a single thought,
Two hearts that beat as one.

And whence comes Love? Like morning bright
Love comes without thy call.

And how dies Love? A spirit bright,
Love never dies at all.

I'd Like

Unknown

I'd like the memory of me to be a happy one.
I'd like to leave an afterglow of smiles when life is done.

I'd like to leave an echo whispering softly down the ways,
of happy times, laughing times and bright and sunny days.

I'd like the tears of those who grieve,
to dry before the sun of happy memories that I leave,
when life is done.

Funeral Blues

W.H. Auden 1907 – 1973
English born American Poet

Stop all the clocks, cut off the telephone,
Prevent the dog from barking with a juicy bone,

Silence the pianos and with muffled drum
Bring out the coffin, let the mourners come.

Let aeroplanes circle moaning overhead
Scribbling on the sky the message He Is Dead,

Put the crepe bows round the necks of the public doves,
Let the traffic policemen wear black cotton gloves.

He was my North, my South, my East and West,
My working week and my Sunday rest,

My noon, my midnight, my talk, my song;
I thought that love would last forever: I was wrong.

The stars are not wanted now: put out every one;
Pack up the moon and dismantle the sun;

Pour away the ocean and sweep up the wood.
For nothing now can ever come to any good.

Desiderata

Max Ehrmann 1872 – 1945
American Lawyer and Poet

Go placidly amid the noise and haste,
and remember what peace there may be in silence.

As far as possible, without surrender,
be on good terms with all persons.

Speak your truth quietly and clearly; and listen to others,
even to the dull and ignorant; they too have their story.
Avoid loud and aggressive persons, they are vexations to the spirit.

If you compare yourself to others, you may become vain and bitter,
for always there will be greater and lesser persons than yourself.
Enjoy your achievements as well as your plans.

Keep interested in your own career, however humble;
it is a real possession in the changing fortunes of time.
Exercise caution in your business affairs, for the world is full of trickery.

But let this not blind you to what virtue there is;
Many persons strive for high ideals,
and everywhere life is full of heroism.

Be yourself.
Especially do not feign affection.
Neither be cynical about love;
for in the face of all aridity and disenchantment
it is as perennial as the grass.

Take kindly the counsel of the years,
gracefully surrendering the things of youth.

Nurture strength of spirit to shield you in sudden misfortune.
But do not distress yourself with dark imaginings.
Many fears are born of fatigue and loneliness.

Beyond a wholesome discipline, be gentle with yourself.
You are a child of the universe no less than the trees and the stars;
you have a right to be here.

And whether or not it is clear to you,
no doubt the universe is unfolding as it should.

Therefore be at peace with God,
whatever you conceive Him to be.

And whatever your labours and aspirations,
in the noisy confusion of life,
keep peace with your soul.

With all its sham, drudgery and broken dreams,
it is still a beautiful world.

Be cheerful.
Strive to be happy.

When We Remember

Unknown

You can shed tears that she is gone
or you can smile because she has lived.

You can close your eyes and pray that she'll come back
or you can open your eyes and see all she's left.

Your heart can be empty because you can't see her
or you can be full of the love you shared.

You can turn your back on tomorrow and live yesterday
or you can be happy for tomorrow because of yesterday.

You can remember her and only that she's gone
or you can cherish her memory and let it live on.

You can cry and close your mind, be empty and turn your back
or you can do what she'd want:
smile,
open your eyes,
love
and go on.

A Ship Sails

From "Toilers of the Sea"
Victor Hugo 1862 – 1926
French Author, exiled to Guernsey

I am standing upon that foreshore.
A ship at my side spreads her white sails in the morning breeze
and starts for the blue ocean.

She is an object of beauty and strength
and I stand and watch her
until at length she hangs like a speck of white cloud
just where the sea and sky come down to mingle with each other.

Then someone at my side says:
"There! She is gone!"

"Gone where?"

"Gone from my sight, that is all."

She is just as large in mast and spar and hull
As ever she was when she left my side;
just as able to bear her load of living freight to the place of her destination.

Her diminished size is in me, not in her.

And just at that moment, when someone at my side says
"There! She is gone!"
there are other eyes watching her coming
and other voices ready to take up the glad shout –

"Here she comes!"

Indian Prayer

Traditional

When I am dead
Cry for me a little
Think of me sometimes

But not too much.

Think of me now and again
As I was in life
At some moments it's pleasant to recall

But not for long.

Leave me in peace
And I shall leave you in peace

And while you live,
Let your thoughts be with the living.

Do Not Stand at My Grave and Weep

Mary Frye 1905 – 2004
American Housewife and Poet

Do not stand at my grave and weep,
I am not there, I do not sleep.

I am a thousand winds that blow,
I am the diamond glints on snow,

I am the sunlight and ripened grain.
I am the gentle Autumn rain.

When you awake in the morning hush,
I am the swift upflinging rush

Of quiet birds in circling flight.
I am the soft star shine at night.

Do not stand at my grave and cry,
I am not there, I did not die.

To My Dear and Loving Husband

Anne Bradstreet 1612 – 1672
American Puritan Poet, born in England

If ever two were one then surely we.
If ever man were loved by wife, then thee;

If ever wife were happy in a man,
Compare with me, ye women, if you can.

I prize thy love more than whole mines of gold
Or all the riches that the East doth hold.

My love is such that rivers cannot quench,
Nor aught but love from thee give recompense.

Thy love is such I can no way repay,
The heavens reward thee manifold, I pray.

Then while we live, in love let's so persevere
That when we live no more, we may live ever.

Do Not Go Gentle into That Good Night

Dylan Thomas 1914 – 1953
Welsh Poet

Do not go gentle into that good night,
Old age should burn and rave at close of day;
Rage, rage against the dying of the light.

Though wise men at their end know dark is right,
Because their words had forked no lightning they
Do not go gentle into that good night.

Good men, the last wave by, crying how bright
Their frail deeds might have danced in a green bay,
Rage, rage against the dying of the light.

Wild men who caught and sang the sun in flight,
And learn, too late, they grieved it on its way,
Do not go gentle into that good night.

Grave men, near death, who see with blinding sight
Blind eyes could blaze like meteors and be gay,
Rage, rage against the dying of the light.

And you, my father, there on the sad height,
Curse, bless, me now with your fierce tears, I pray.
Do not go gentle into that good night.
Rage, rage against the dying of the light.

If I Should Go

Unknown

If I should go tomorrow
It would never be goodbye,
For I have left my heart with you,
So don't you ever cry.

The love that's deep within me,
Shall reach you from the stars,
You'll feel it from the heavens,
And it will heal the scars.

I Have Seen Death Too Often

Unknown

I have seen death too often
To believe in death:

For it is like arriving at the end of the day,
Turning off the engine, switching off the lights,
And gently closing the car door;

Then walking up the path, up to the steps
And into the light of home.

Young Life Cut Short – For the Brother of My Friend

Unknown

Do not judge a biography by its length,
Nor by the number of pages in it.

Judge it by the richness of it's contents

Sometimes those unfinished are among the most poignant…

Do not judge a song by its duration
Nor by the number of its notes

Judge it by the way it touches and lifts the soul

Sometimes those unfinished are among the most beautiful…

And when something has enriched your life
And when it's melody lingers on in your heart

Is it unfinished?

Or is it endless?

I'll Be There

Maude Hurford
Guernsey Poet

I've come to the end of life's busy road
I've put down my burden, I've cast off my load

My spirit is free, my soul has wings
I'll pour from the throat of a bird that sings

I'll ride on the wind, I'll float on the clouds
I'll twinkle with the stars in night's velvet shroud

I'll shine with the sun as it circles the earth
I'll be there at the dawn when a new day gives birth

I'll be with the snow fluttering down
Silently, softly, nature's crown

I'll be in the rain as it falls on the earth
Cleansing, refreshing, priceless worth

I'll ride on the ether, silent and free
A world of my own, please don't cry for me

Come To Me

Unknown

God saw you getting tired
and a cure was not to be
so he put his arms around you
and whispered,
"Come to Me"

With tearful eyes we watch you
and saw you pass away
and although we loved you dearly
we could not make you stay.

A Golden heart stopped beating
hard working hands at rest.
God broke our hearts to prove us
he only takes the best

When You Are Old

W.B. Yeats 1865 - 1939
Irish Dramatist and Poet

When you are old and grey and full of sleep,
And nodding by the fire, take down this book,

And slowly read, and dream of the soft look
Your eyes had once, and of their shadows deep;

How many loved your moments of glad grace,
And loved your beauty with love false or true,

But one man loved the pilgrim soul in you,
And loved the sorrows of your changing face;

And bending down beside the glowing bars,
Murmur, a little sadly, how Love fled

And paced upon the mountains overhead
And hid his face amid a crowd of stars.

Break, Break, Break

Lord Alfred Tennyson 1809 – 1892
English Royal Poet Laureate for 40 years

Break, break, break
On thy cold grey stones, O Sea!
And I would that my tongue could utter
The thoughts that arise in me.

O well for the fisherman's boy,
That he shouts with his sister at play!
O well for the sailor lad,
That he sings in his boat on the bay!

And the stately ships go on
To their haven under the hill;
But O for the touch of a vanish'd hand,
And the sound of a voice that is still!

Break, break, break
At the foot of the crags, O Sea!
But the tender grace of a day that is dead
Will never come back to me.

From "Little Women"

Louisa May Alcott 1832 – 1888
American Novelist

Beth could not reason upon
or explain the faith
that gave her courage and patience to give up life,
and cheerfully wait for death.

Like a confiding child, she asked no questions,
but left everything to God and nature,
Father and Mother of us all,
feeling sure that they, and they only,
could teach and strengthen heart and spirit for this life
and the life to come.

To All Parents

Edgar Guest 1881 – 1959
American Poet

"I'll lend you for a little time a child of mine," He said.
"For you to love the while he lives and mourn when he is dead,

"It may be six or seven years, or twenty-two or three,
"But will you, till I call him back, take care of him for me?

"He'll bring his charms to gladden you, but should his stay be brief,
"You'll have his lovely memories, as solace for your grief,

"I cannot promise he will stay, since all from earth return,
"But there are lessons taught down there I want this child to learn.

"I've looked the wide world over in my search for teachers true,
"And from the throngs that crowd life's lanes I have selected you.

"Now will you give him all your love, nor think the labor vain,
"Nor hate me when I come to call to take him back again?

I fancied that I heard them say: "Dear Lord, Thy will be done!
"For all the joy Thy child shall bring, the risk of grief we'll run.

We'll shelter him with tenderness; we'll love him while we may,
And for happiness we've known forever grateful stay.

"But should the angels call for him much sooner than we'd planned,
"We'll brave the bitter grief that comes and try to understand."

My Love

Claribel Alegria 1924 –
Nicaraguan Poet, translated by Carolyn Forché

Give me your hand my love
don't let me sink into sadness.

My body has already learned
the grief of your absence
but despite the blows
it still wants to live.

Don't go away
love
meet me in my dreams
defend your memory
my memory of you
that I don't want to lose.

We are voice and echo
mirror and face
give me your hand

Wait
I have to rearrange my time
until I reach you

Up-Hill

Christina Rossetti 1830 – 1894
English Poet

Does the road wind up-hill all the way?
Yes, to the very end.

Will the day's journey take the whole long day?
From morn to night, my friend.

But is there for the night a resting-place?
A roof for when the slow dark hours begin.

May not the darkness hide it from my face?
You cannot miss that inn.

Shall I meet other wayfarers at night?
Those who have gone before.

Then must I knock, or call when just in sight?
They will not keep you standing at that door.

Shall I find comfort, travel-sore and weak?
Of labour you shall find the sum.

Will there be beds for me and all who seek?
Yea, beds for all who come.

Death, Where Is Thy Sting?

From "The Pilgrim's Progress"
John Bunyan 1628 – 1688
English Preacher and Writer

Then said he, "I am going to my Father's,
and though with great difficulty I am going hither,
yet now I do not repent me of all the trouble I have been at,
to arrive where I am.

My sword I give to him that shall succeed me in my pilgrimage,
and my courage and skill to him that can get it.

My marks and scars I carry with me, to be a witness for me,
that I have fought His battles, who now will be my rewarder."

When the day that he must go hence was come,
many accompanied him to the riverside,
into which as he went he said
"Death, where is thy sting?"

And as he went down deeper, he said
"Grave, where is thy victory?"

So, he passed over,
and all the trumpets sounded for him on the other side.

All Is Well

Henry Scott Holland 1847 – 1918
Canon of St Paul's Cathedral, London

Death is nothing at all,
I have only slipped into the next room

I am I and you are you
Whatever we were to each other, that we are still.

Call me by my old familiar name,
Speak to me in the easy way which you always used
Put no difference in your tone,
Wear no forced air of solemnity or sorrow

Laugh as we always laughed at the little jokes we enjoyed together.
Play, smile, think of me, pray for me.

Let my name be ever the household world that it always was,
Let it be spoken without effect, without the trace of shadow on it.

Life means all that it ever meant.
It is the same as it ever was, there is unbroken continuity.

Why should I be out of mind because I am out of sight?

I am waiting for you, for an interval, somewhere very near,
Just around the corner.

All is well.

Death Cannot Kill What Never Dies

From "Fruits of Solitude" Part II Union of Friends
William Penn 1644 – 1718
Quaker Theologist and Founder of Pennsylvania

They that love beyond the world cannot be separated by it.
Death cannot kill what never dies.

Nor can spirits ever be divided
That love and live in the same divine principle:
the root and record of their friendship.

Death is but a crossing the world as friends do seas;
they live in one another still.

For they must needs be present
that love and live in that which is omnipresent.

In this Divine glass they see face to face;
and their converse is free as well as pure.

This is the comfort of friends,
that though they may be said to die,
yet their friendship and society are, in the best sense,
ever present,
because immortal.

Speak to Us of Joy and Sorrow

Kahlil Gibran 1883 – 1931
Lebanese Poet and Artist, died USA

Then a woman said, "Speak to us of Joy and Sorrow."
And He answered:

"Your joy is your sorrow unmasked.
And the selfsame well from which your laughter rises was oftentimes filled with your tears.

And how else can it be?

The deeper your sorrow carves into your being,
the more joy you can contain.

Is not the cup that holds your wine
the very cup that was burned in the potter's oven?

And is not the lute that soothes your spirit
the very wood that was hollowed by knives?

When you are joyous,
look deep into your heart and you shall find
it is only that which has given you sorrow
that is giving you joy."

Divine Love Cannot Change

From "War and Peace"
Leo Tolstoy 1828 – 1910
Russian Novelist and Activist

Loving with human love,
one may pass from love to hatred;
but divine love cannot change.

Nothing, not even death, can shatter it.
It is the very nature of the soul...
Love is life.

All, all that I understand,
I understand only because I love.

All is bound up in love alone.
Love is God,
and dying means for me a particle of love,
to go back to the universal and eternal source of love.

'Tis Better to Have Loved

Lord Alfred Tennyson 1809 – 1892
English Royal Poet Laureate for 40 years

I envy not in any moods
the captive void of noble rage,
the linnet born within the cage
that never knew the summer woods:

I envy not the beast that takes
his license in the field of time,
unfetter'd by the sense of crime,
to whom a conscience never wakes;

Nor, what may count itself as blest,
the heart that never plighted troth
but stagnates in the weeds of sloth,
nor any want-begotten rest.

I hold it true, whate'er befall;
I feel it when I sorrow most;
'Tis better to have loved and lost
Than never to have loved at all.

When I Am Gone

Unknown

When I am gone release me,
Let me go, I have so many things to see and do.

You mustn't tie yourself to me with tears,
Be happy that we had so many beautiful years

I gave to you my love.
You can only guess how much you gave me in happiness.

I thank you for the love you each have shown,
But now it's time I travel alone.

So grieve for me a while, if you must
Then let your grief be comforted by my trust.

It's only for a while we must part,
So bless the memories in your heart.

I won't be far away, for life carries on,
So if you need me, call and I will come.

Though you can't see or touch me, I'll be near.
And if you listen within your heart you'll hear

All my love around you soft and clear.
And then when you must come this way alone

I'll greet you with a smile and say
"Welcome Home"

On Death

Kahlil Gibran 1883 – 1931
Lebanese Poet and Artist, died USA

You would know the secret of death.
But how shall you find it unless you seek it in the heart of life?

The owl whose night-bound eyes are blind unto the day
cannot unveil the mystery of light.
If you would indeed behold the spirit of death,
open your heart wide unto the body of life.

For life and death are one,
even as the river and the sea are one.
In the depth of your hopes and desires
lies your silent knowledge of the beyond;

And like seeds dreaming beneath the snow
your heart dreams of spring.
Trust the dreams,
for in them is hidden the gate to eternity.

For what is it to die
but to stand naked in the wind and to melt into the sun?
And what is it to cease breathing,
but to free the breath from its restless tides,
that it may rise and expand and seek God unencumbered?

Only when you drink from the river of silence shall you indeed sing.
And when you have reached the mountain top,
then you shall begin to climb.
And when the earth shall claim your limbs,
then shall you truly dance.

You'll Never Walk Alone

From "Carousel"
Oscar Hammerstein 11 1895 – 1960
American Writer and Musical Director

When you walk through the storm
Hold your head up high,
And don't be afraid of the dark

At the end of the storm
is a golden sky
And the sweet silver song of a lark.

Walk on through the wind,
Walk on through the rain,
Though your dreams be tossed and blown

Walk on, walk on,
With hope in your heart
And you'll never walk alone

You'll never walk alone.

Not How Did He Die

Unknown

Not how did he die, but how did he live?

Not what did he gain, but what did he give?

These are the units to measure the worth
Of a man as a man, regardless of birth.

Not what was his church, or what was his creed,
But had he befriended those really in need?

Not what was his station, but had he a heart?
How did he play in his God-given part?

Was he ever ready, with words of good cheer,
To bring back a smile, to banish a tear?

Not how did the formal obituary run,

But how many grieved when his life's work was done?

The Lord is My Shepherd

From the CHRISTIAN BIBLE
Psalm 23

The Lord is my shepherd, I shall not want.

He makes me lie down in green pastures,
He leads me beside quiet waters,
He restores my soul.
He guides me in paths of righteousness for His name's sake.

Even though I walk through the valley of the shadow of death,
I will fear no evil, for you are with me;
Your rod and your staff, they comfort me.

You prepare a table before me in the presence of my enemies.
You anoint my head with oil; my cup overflows.

Surely goodness and love will follow me all the days of my life,
And I will dwell in the house of the Lord forever.

I Am the Bread of Life

From the CHRISTIAN BIBLE
John 6:35-40

Jesus said to them,
'I am the bread of life.
Whoever comes to me will never be hungry,
and whoever believes in me will never be thirsty.

But I said to you that you have seen me and yet do not believe.
Everything that the Father gives me will come to me,
and anyone who comes to me I will never drive away;

For I have come down from heaven,
not to do my own will,
but the will of him who sent me.

And this is the will of him who sent me,
that I should lose nothing of all that he has given me,
but raise it up on the last day.

This is indeed the will of my Father,
that all who see the Son and believe in him may have eternal life;
and I will raise them up on the last day.'

Look to This Day!

From the SANSKRIT (Hindu and Buddhist texts)

Look to this day!
For it is life, the very life of life.

In its brief course lie all the varieties and realities of your existence:
the bliss of growth,
the glory of action,
the splendour of beauty.

For yesterday is already a dream,
and tomorrow is only a vision,

But today, well-lived,
makes every yesterday a dream of happiness,
and every tomorrow a vision of hope.

Look well, therefore, to this day!
Such is the salutation of the dawn.

The Greatest of These is Love

From the CHRISTIAN BIBLE
Corinthians 1:13

If I speak in the tongues of men and of angels,
but have not love,
I am a noisy gong or a clanging cymbal.

And if I have the prophetic powers,
and understand all mysteries and all knowledge,
and if I have all faith, so as to remove mountains,
but have not love,
I am nothing.

If I give away all I have,
and if I deliver my body to be burned,
but have not love,
I gain nothing.

Love is patient, love is kind;
Love is not jealous, or boastful; it is not arrogant or rude.
Love does not insist on its own way;
it is not irritable or resentful;
it does not rejoice at wrong, but rejoices in right.

Love bears all things, believes all things,
hopes all things, endures all things.

Love never ends;
As for prophesies, they will pass away
As for tongues, they will cease
As for knowledge, it will pass away.
For our knowledge is imperfect and our prophecy is imperfect;
But when the perfect comes, the imperfect will pass away.
When I was a child,
I spoke like a child, I thought like a child, I reasoned like a child;
When I became a man,
I gave up the childish ways.

For now we see in a mirror dimly,
but then face-to-face.

Now I know in part;
then I shall understand fully,
even as I have been fully understood.

There are three things that last forever –
Faith
Hope and
Love

But the greatest of these is love.

I Am Making All Things New

From the CHRISTIAN BIBLE
Revelation 21:1-7

I, John, saw a new heaven and a new earth;
for the first heaven and the first earth had passed away,
and the sea was no more.

And I saw the holy city, the new Jerusalem,
coming down out of heaven from God,
prepared as a bride adorned for her husband.
And I heard a loud voice from the throne saying,

'See, the home of God is among mortals.
He will dwell with them;
they will be his peoples,
and God himself will be with them;
he will wipe every tear from their eyes.
Death will be no more;
mourning and crying and pain will be no more,
for the first things have passed away.'

And the one who was seated on the throne said,
'See, I am making all things new.'

Also he said, '
Write this, for these words are trustworthy and true.'
Then he said to me,
'It is done!
I am the Alpha and the Omega, the beginning and the end.
To the thirsty I will give water as a gift from the spring of the water of life.
Those who conquer will inherit these things,
and I will be their God and they will be my children.'

Lord, We Turn to You

From the JEWISH FUNERAL SERVICE PRAYER BOOK

Lord, we turn to you in our grief and bewilderment,
for a mystery surrounds the birth and death of man.

Your will summons us into this world and then calls us to depart,
but Your plan is so vast and Your purposes so deep
that our understanding fails, and our reason cannot follow.

Yet You have taught us that time and space are not the measure
of all things.
Beyond them is the life of eternity.
We do not die into the grave but into the love of God.

It has been Your will to receive the soul of him/her,
to bring him/her to the life everlasting,
and she/he is beyond the tragedies of this world.

We shall find our comfort in Your teaching.
Beyond the grave we shall meet together
in the life that has no end.

A Time For All Things

From the CHRISTIAN BIBLE
Ecclesiastes 3:1-8

For everything there is a season,
And a time for every matter under heaven:

A time to be born, and a time to die;
A time to plant, and a time to pluck up what is planted;
A time to kill, and a time to heal;

A time to break down, and a time to build up;
A time to weep, and a time to laugh;

A time to mourn, and a time to dance;
A time to throw away stones, and a time to gather stones together;

A time to embrace, And a time to refrain from embracing;
A time to seek, and a time to lose;

A time to keep, and a time to throw away;
A time to tear, and a time to sew;

A time to keep silence, and a time to speak;
A time to love, and a time to hate,

A time for war, and a time for peace.

Shorter Quotes

From the CHRISTIAN BIBLE

'I am the resurrection and the life,' says the Lord. 'Those who believe in me, even though they die, will live, and everyone who lives and believes in me will never die.'

John 11.25-26

I am convinced that neither death, nor life, nor angels, nor rulers, nor things present, nor things to come, nor powers, nor height, nor depth, nor anything else in all creation, will be able to separate us
from the love of God in Christ Jesus our Lord.

Romans 8.38-39

Since we believe that Jesus died and rose again, even so, through Jesus,
God will bring with him those who have died.
So we will be with the Lord for ever.
Therefore encourage one another with these words.

1 Thessalonians 4.14,17b,18

We brought nothing into the world, and we take nothing out.
The Lord gave, and the Lord has taken away;
blessed be the name of the Lord.

1 Timothy 6.7; Job 1.21b

The steadfast love of the Lord never ceases, his mercies never come to an end;
they are new every morning; great is his faithfulness.

Lamentations 3.22-23

Blessed are those who mourn, for they will be comforted.

Matthew 5.4

God so loved the world that he gave his only Son, so that everyone who believes in him may not perish but may have eternal life.

John 3.16

Chapter 10 Music for Listening and Singing

It has been with us since time began,
and it is important in every country
and culture across the world.

All of the major events in our societies
are accompanied by it,
and the more grand the event the
more pivotal and powerful it becomes.

It can make us laugh, cry, dance, sleep or dream.
We can be inspired to love like never before,
to fight battles with renewed courage,
to accept that which we cannot change,
to forgive and reflect,
or simply to remember another time.

Music is the language of our souls and our emotions.
It expresses that which has no words.
It reaches across countries,
ages and language boundaries,
and instantly unites us in purpose.

Never underestimate the power of music.

Music Before, During and After a Funeral

Every gathering will have a beginning, a middle and an end. There is a natural flow of events to keep in mind when planning what will take place.

Just as the spoken word will move us through the various stages of a gathering, music will play an equally important role.

Before the Funeral

As people arrive, it is very easy to create a sense of occasion and a "sacred space" by playing music. It also encourages people to gather close, and helps to declare our common purpose. There is a third reason to have music before a funeral – when the music stops it announces quite naturally that it is time to cease any conversation and begin the funeral.

A good general rule is to avoid songs with words (particularly in English) as our ear will be naturally drawn to them. The aim is for the music to create an atmosphere, not to compete for the mourner's attention with greetings and other conversations.

Emotions in the music could include respect, calmness and dignity.

During the Funeral

There are many possibilities for the role of music during a funeral. The music you choose could –

- Create a reflective background, allowing mourners the space to quietly consider their own thoughts and memories of the person that has died

- Uphold and confirm a particular unifying religious belief or custom

- Speak to those present of the emotions of grief, of sadness, of hope, of peace

- Represent the person that has died, either as a description of their character or lifestyle, or simply as one of their favourite songs.

The beginning and end of a funeral service are quite different, but both try to create a feeling of comfort and unity.

It is in the middle of a funeral that we often find the vulnerability of loss most freely expressed, held within the safety of a common and protective gathering.

If you have chosen any particularly sad music, then it should be placed in the middle of the funeral.

When we are first mourning the death of someone we love, our emotions will vary greatly. Each day, each hour will bring new feelings and perspectives on what has happened. Resist the temptation to play only very sad, or only joyous music.

If we are to truly remember the person that has died in a meaningful way, then both emotions may exist. Consider others that are mourning with you, and try to represent a good cross-section of the emotions that may be present.

We may be happy that they have lived, but we are sad that they have gone.

After the Funeral

The choice for the final piece of music is an important one.

- If you want to uplift the gathering, then now is the time to rejoice that someone has lived
- If you want to quietly reflect on the beauty of life and the bittersweet inevitability of death, then choose music that maintains dignity
- If you want to confirm your faith in a religious belief, then announce your praises loudly

There are no rules for how a funeral should end, however your music must allow people to rejoin their daily lives in the world outside.

If your piece of music is a song with words, then you can almost guarantee these words will be in their ears for many hours, or even days, to come.

Live Music and Resources

- Many traditional religious funerals will have sung prayers or a selection of hymns. If you find that your religious leader indicates that only certain music should be used, then you can take comfort in the tradition of families past and allow the music to represent your strong faith and belief.

- Some people prefer to integrate other choices into certain parts of a traditional ceremony, and this can work very well, in consultation with the service leader.

- If you are creating a more secular or non-traditional funeral, then your choice of music is yours completely. It may be one of the most effective ways that you can represent the character and individuality of the deceased person.

Your choice of musicians will provide a very important function in determining what music may be performed on the day.

I sat in the front row of my grandmother's funeral.
As a professional musician, perhaps I should have led the singing loudest of all. Instead, I found myself silent, completely enveloped in the sound of everyone behind me, singing and remembering together.

I had never heard a sweeter, more comforting sound.
I was cushioned and magically protected in the circle of community that touched me as never before.

It stays with me to this day, the feeling of unity and purpose that words could never express.

Organists and pianists will almost certainly need an instrument to be present at the venue. At the very least they will need access to power if they are to bring their own keyboard and amplification.

It can sometimes be difficult to get a competent organist for a funeral as many will hold week-day jobs. Do check that they are up to the task of playing any music you have selected. If they are not, they will usually say so and suggest worthwhile alternatives to the pieces you had chosen.

Singers will normally not use a microphone unless they are outside, and even then only if it is very noisy or a large number of people are present. Sometimes asking a family friend to sing can be a wonderful alternative. Many religious leaders and funeral celebrants are reasonably confidant singers and are trained to lead groups in singing at a gathering.

The act of group singing is often very powerful, and can provide great comfort to those present.

Sometimes unusual instruments can be the perfect choice for a funeral. Examples include solo trumpet, bagpipes, or a children's choir.

When considering live music, remember that –

- Some pieces can be performed by many people, in slightly different ways each time, and the piece will remain unchanged and quite acceptable overall
- Some pieces are popular and well-known only in their original version, by the original performer that recorded them.

Be sure you will be satisfied with the new version of a well-known piece normally associated with one particular performer.

Recorded Music

One of the ways that we can remember someone best is by bringing the music of our daily lives into a funeral.

Think carefully about the choice of contemporary, commercial music for a farewell. Do not go ahead unless you are sure that it will definitely be appropriate on the day.

Please consider not only your reaction but the reaction of others as you all meet together to remember. Sometimes a piece of music that seems to be a good choice when thinking about a tribute turns out to be inappropriate when the actual day arrives. Perhaps discuss your selection with others.

Be sure to listen fully to all the words, you may be surprised at what you hear when you are studying lyrics. Remember that people who may not have heard your song will assume there is a message in it for them – and they will listen intently to find it.

If you are absolutely sure, then embrace your choice of music and enjoy the individual tribute it will invariably create.

If you are going to burn a CD compilation to use on the day, check that your CD will play in at least two different music players. It can also be a good idea to bring the original CDs with you, just in case there are problems on the day.

Sometimes it is possible to have somebody play through your music on the actual player that will be used, at the location of the funeral.

Write down the volume levels at which it sounds best. Leave clear instructions inside the CD cover for the person that will operate the music.

Notice how loud and how clear it is, and remember that when you place many people inside a room that the sound will not have as much echo and will be a little softer in the areas furthest from the speakers.

Don't be afraid to change your selection if necessary. Internet shops such as iTunes mean that music can be sourced quite easily and quickly. Below are some suggestions for recorded music that may be suitable for a funeral.

1930

Good Night Sweetheart	Guy Lombardo (also Rudy Vallee 1960)
It's Easy to Remember	Bing Crosby
Side By Side	Traditional (try Mitch Miller)
They Can't Take That Away From Me	Peggy Lee (also Frank Sinatra)

1940

I'll Be Seeing You	Bing Crosby
Now Is the Hour	Bing Crosby
Sentimental Journey	Doris Day
Somewhere Over the Rainbow	Judy Garland
Till the End of Time	Perry Como
We'll Meet Again	Vera Lyn

1950

All I Have to Do is Dream	Everley Brothers
Because of You	Tony Bennett
Harbour Lights	The Platters
My Way	Frank Sinatra
Too Young	Nat King Cole
What a Wonderful World	Louis Armstrong

1960

Comes a Time	Neil Young
Dream a Little Dream of Me	The Mamas & The Papas
Forever Young	Bob Dylan
In My Life	The Beatles
Let It Be	The Beatles
Stand By Me	Ben E King
Try to Remember (September)	Nana Mouskouri
Unchained Melody	Righteous Brothers (Used in the movie "Ghost")
You'll Never Walk Alone	Gerry & the Pacemakers

1970

As Long As I Can See the Light	Creedence Clearwater Revival
Always Look on the Bright Side	Monty Python
Bridge Over Troubled Water	Simon & Garfunkel
Bright Eyes	Simon & Garfunkel
Candle In The Wind	Elton John (Later changed for Princess Diana)
Evergreen	Barbara Streisand
Fire and Rain (See You Again)	James Taylor
Goodbye My Friend	Linda Rondstat
Hymn	Barclay James Harvest
Imagine	John Lennon
The Rose	Bette Midler
The Way We Were	Barbara Streisand
Time in a Bottle	Jim Croce
When I Get Where I' m Going	Brad Paisley & Dolly Parton
You've Got a Friend	James Taylor

1980

Baby Mine	Bette Midler (from movie "Beaches)
Carry Me (Like a Fire in your Heart)	Chris deBurgh
Dance with My Father	Luther Vandross
Don't Worry Be Happy	Bobby McFerrin
Downstream	Supertramp
Everything I Do	Bryan Adams
I've Had The Time Of My Life	Jennifer Warnes & Bill Medley
Lean on Me	Club Nouveau
Lullaby	Billy Joel
Simply the Best	Tina Turner
Time After Time	Cyndi Lauper
That's What Friends Are For	Dionne Warwick
True Colors	Cyndi Lauper
Wind Beneath My Wings	Bette Midler

1990

Angels	Robbie Williams
Because You Loved Me	Celine Dion
Con Te Partiro / Say Goodbye	Andrea Bocelli & Sarah Brightman
The Dance	Garth Brooks
The Day You Went Away	Wendy Matthews
Everybody Hurts	REM
Fields of Gold	Eva Cassidy (Very reflective)
Fields of Gold	Sting (More straightforward)
Fly	Celine Dion
Hard to Say Goodbye	Boyz 2 Men
I Don't Want to Miss a Thing	Aerosmith
If I Could Be Where You Are	Enya
If I Had Only Known	Reba McEntire
If Tomorrow Never Comes	Ronan Keating
I'm Your Angel	Celine Dion & R Kelly
I Will Always Love You	Whitney Houston (or Dolly Parton – probably a better version for a funeral)
My Heart Will Go On	Celine Dion (From the movie "Titanic")
Never Tear Us Apart	INXS
New Years Day	U2
People Get Ready	Eva Cassidy
Somewhere Over the Rainbow	Eva Cassidy
Tears In Heaven	Eric Clapton
Thankyou for the Memories	Rod Stewart
Time To Say Goodbye	Sarah Brightman
Together Again	Janet Jackson
With Or Without You	U2
You Are Not Alone	Michael Jackson
You Were Loved	Whitney Houston

2000

Bittersweet Symphony	The Verve
Circle of Life	Elton John
Falling Into You	Kasey Chambers
Goodbye My Lover	James Blunt
If Only I Could Make Heaven Wait	Guy Sebastian
If We Never Meet Again	Selah
I'll Be Missing You	Puff Daddy
In the Arms of the Angels	Sarah McLachlann
I Will Remember You	Sarah McLachlan
Just Around the River Bend	From Pocahontas
Million Tears	Kasey Chambers
My Immortal	Evanescence
One Sweet Day	Mariah Carey & Boyz 2 Men
Slipped Away	Avril Lavigne
Superman	Five for Fighting
There You'll Be	Faith Hill
Time of Your Life	Green Day
To Where You Are	Josh Gorban
Who Knew	Female US
World's Greatest	R Kelly
You Raise Me Up	Westlife

Pop Music Summary

- Be sure to listen fully to all the words, you may be surprised at what you hear when you are studying lyrics.
- Remember that we all grieve differently. If possible try to include as many people as possible, not exclude those who may not be familiar with the music.
- Remember that people who may not have heard your song will assume there is a message in it for them – and they will listen intently to find it.
- Some songs work very well performed live, which will always have a slightly different sound or style. Other songs are best left to the original recording.

Hymns and other Ceremonial Music

The Christian faith has a long tradition of hymns to select from when planning for a funeral. These hymns will usually work equally well in a Church, or a Funeral Director's premises, or even at an outside location.

On **'When We Remember'** CD are the following recordings –

16 The Lord is My Shepherd
17 Going Home (Christ Gone Before)
18 Abide With Me
19 Going Home (Live in Me)
20 Amazing Grace (Choir)

All of these would be suitable for a funeral service, and have been recorded in such a way to ensure they are excellent to sing along with.

Even if you are unsure as to your Christian beliefs, these hymns may be just what you are looking for as they perfectly capture many elements common to all who grieve.

When selecting a hymn, be sure to check fully all of the words to be used. Many traditional hymns will have several verses and you may wish to omit any verses that you do not feel are appropriate at this time.

There are many reasons why we have recorded these hymns –

- Sometimes a funeral is to be held during the week, or in a less populated area, and we are unable to find an organist or other musicians to play the music we would like.

- Perhaps we are paying tribute to the Christian faith of a relative by holding a funeral in church, but do not attend church ourselves. The five hymns selected are popular, appropriate, and have been recorded in keys that are easy to sing.

- The hymn versions have been recorded with the specific occasion of a funeral in mind. The tempo, instrumentation, style and recording techniques have been chosen to be as suitable and welcoming as possible – encouraging people to sing or at very least feel included as they listen to the music.

Sometimes hymns are selected by words alone, and there may be two or more melodies that can be used for these words. Be sure to check with the person who is to lead the gathering or singing as to which tune they are expecting to use.

It will encourage confidence and provide more comfort if people have a reasonably well known melody sing to.

If you are not generally familiar with hymns, you may be very surprised with the familiarity of the well known tunes of many of the hymns listed below.

There is a centuries old tradition of dividing the church devotional day into specific periods of time.

Many of these hymns come from the period known as Evensong – praise and acknowledgement for the day that had been.

Consider –

- All Things Bright and Beautiful
- And Can It Be
- Be Still My Soul
- Be Thou My Vision
- The Day Thou Gavest Lord, is Ended
- Eternal Father, Strong to Save
- God of Our Fathers
- Great is Thy Faithfulness
- Guide Me, O Thou Great Redeemer
- Here I Am Lord
- How Great Thou Art
- Jerusalem
- The King of Love My Shepherd Is
- Lead Us, Heavenly Father
- Lord of All Hopefulness
- Lord of the Dance
- Make Me a Channel of Your Peace
- Morning Has Broken
- Nearer My God to Thee
- O God, Our Help in Ages Past
- The Old Rugged Cross
- Our Eyes Have Seen the Glory
- Praise My Soul, the King of Heaven
- Swing Low, Sweet Chariot
- Thine Be the Glory
- To God be the Glory, Great Things He Hath Done
- What a Friend We Have in Jesus

Classical Music for Atmosphere or Reflection

'When We Remember' contains a selection of "classical" music that would be suitable to use before or after a funeral, and also as a background for reflection during a memorial gathering.

Even if you are familiar with classical music, it can sometimes be very difficult to remember the titles of music that you would like, or to find good versions of a particular piece that you would like to use.

Sometimes we enjoy a particular short melody, only to find when an excerpt of a few minutes is played, that the music wanders off into another melody that is no longer suitable.

You will probably have heard many of these melodies before, but may not know the title or composer of the piece you have listened to. It can be very surprising to realise just how much classical music is used in movies, radio and television. Even unlikely moments such as sporting events or gardening shows are greatly enhanced by the music of the centuries-old masters. There is an enormous variety of classical music available, and it must be chosen wisely.

Take a few minutes to listen through the CD, you may be pleasantly surprised by the feelings and atmosphere that each one can suggest.

Most of the music on 'When We Remember' is instrumental, allowing listeners to be part of the experience of listening, without actually having sung words drawing our attention away from the thoughts and conversations we may be having at the time.

The vocal selections are simple and contain beautiful melodies – the words are not the main feature and the music remains the main focus when listening.

All of the pieces on 'When We Remember' are around three minutes in length, the same as popular songs that are played on the radio.

‘When We Remember’ Music CD

Instrumental Solos

Solo Piano	“Pathetique” Sonata 2nd Movement	Beethoven
	“Moonlight” Sonata 1st Movement	Beethoven
Solo Organ	“Jesu, Joy of Man’s Desiring”	J S Bach
Solo Guitar	“Prelude No.1”	Villa-Lobos
Solo Bagpipe	Amazing Grace	Traditional
Solo Trumpet	Last Post and Reveille	Traditional

Instrumental Solos with Piano Accompaniment

Flute	“Pavanne”	Faure
Flute and Clarinet	“Sicilienne”	Faure
Cello	“The Swan” from Carnival of the Animals	Saint-Saëns
Violin	“Meditation” from Thais	Massenet

Solos with Organ or Other Accompaniment

Guitar and Strings	“Concerto de Aranjuez”	Rodrigo
Female Voice	“My Redeemer Liveth” from Messiah	Handel
	“Pie Jesu” from Requiem	Faure
Choir	“Ave Verum”	Mozart
String Quartet	“Adagio” in G minor	Albinoni
	“Canon”	Pachelbel
	“Air” from Suite No.3	J S Bach

Abide With Me

Music: "Eventide" William H. Monk, 1861

Abide With Me

Words: Henry F. Lyte, 1847

Abide with me; fast falls the eventide;
The darkness deepens; Lord with me abide.

When other helpers fail and comforts flee,
Help of the helpless, O abide with me.

I fear no foe, with Thee at hand to bless;
Ills have no weight, and tears no bitterness.

Where is death's sting? Where, grave, thy victory?
I triumph still, if Thou abide with me.

Hold Thou Thy cross before my closing eyes;
Shine through the gloom and point me to the skies.

Heaven's morning breaks, and Earth's vain shadows flee;
In life, in death, O Lord, abide with me.

Amazing Grace

Music: Traditional Celtic / Gaelic

Amazing Grace

Words: John Newton 1725 – 1807

Amazing Grace! How sweet the sound
That saved a wretch like me!
I once was lost, but now am found;
Was blind, but now I see.

'Twas Grace that taught my heart to fear,
And Grace my fears relieved;
How precious did that Grace appear
The hour I first believed.

Through many dangers, toils and snares,
I have already come;
'Tis Grace that brought me safe thus far,
And Grace will lead me home.

The Lord has promised good to me,
His word my hope secures;
He will my shield and portion be,
As long as life endures.

When we've been there ten thousand years,
Bright shining as the sun,
We've no less days to sing God's praise
Than when we'd first begun.

Amazing Grace! How sweet the sound
That saved a wretch like me!
I once was lost, but now am found;
Was blind, but now I see.

The Lord's My Shepherd

Music: "Crimond"

The Lord's My Shepherd

Words: Psalm 23 Arr Francis Rous 1579 – 1659

The Lord's my Shepherd, I'll not want;
He makes me down to lie
In pastures green; He leadeth me
The quiet waters by.

My soul He doth restore again
And me to walk doth make
Within the paths of righteousness,
Even for His own name's sake.

Yea, though I walk in death's dark vale
Yet will I fear no ill;
For Thou art with me, and Thy rod
And staff my comfort still.

My table Thou hast furnished me
In presence of my foes;
My head Thou dost with oil anoint,
And my cup overflows.

Goodness and mercy all my life
Shall surely follow me;
And in God's house forevermore,
My dwelling place shall be.

Going Home (You Will Live In Me)

Music: From Dvorak "New World Symphony" 2nd Movt
Arr: J Abraham

Going Home
(You Will Live In Me)

Words: M Abraham

Is it like going home,
When death calls you near?
Hear my voice, feel my love,
Help to dry my tears

Where are you? Near or far? Gone with morning's tide?
Why can I hear you still? Are you by my side?

Set your sail, spirit free,
Earthly cares now gone,
Love remains, strong and clear,
I will carry on

Sorrow stings, heal my pain,
Guide me now in peace,
Comfort me, hold me close,
Fears my tears release

Softly now, close the door, now the day is through,
Every thought, every word, I'll remember you

All we shared still remains,
Let my promise be
Strong and clear, hear my song,
You will live in me

Going Home (Christ Has Gone Before)

Music: From Dvorak "New World Symphony" 2nd Movt
Arr: J Abraham

Going Home
(Christ Has Gone Before)

Words: Unknown

Going home, moving on,
Through God's open door;
Hush my soul, have no fear,
Christ has gone before

Parting hurts, love protests, pain is not denied;
Yet in Christ, love and hope span the great divide

Going home, moving on,
Through God's open door;
Hush my soul, have no fear,
Christ has gone before

No more guilt, no more fear,
All the past is healed;
Broken dreams now restored,
Perfect grace revealed

Christ has died, Christ is ris'n, Christ will come again;
Death destroyed, life restored, love alone shall reign

Going home, moving on,
Through God's open door;
Hush my soul, have no fear,
Christ has gone before

Chapter 11 Technology & Other Meaningful Ideas

When it comes to creating meaningful funerals or memorial gatherings, there are as many choices as there are personalities in the world.

Consider any and all ideas that may appeal. Use the following suggestions to inspire your own unique gathering and rituals. Respect and honour the person that has died, and create meaningful memories for those that remain.

There are many suggestions and ideas throughout this book, and following are listed just a few of the options available.

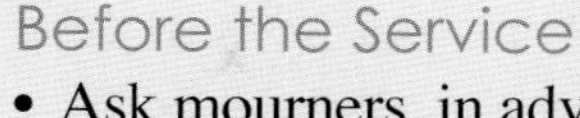

Before the Service

- Ask mourners, in advance, to wear special clothing or bring certain items.

Perhaps there is a favourite colour, or signature hat, or other item of clothing that would be significant for people to wear as they gather. The same applies to photographs, sporting trophies, and many other items that could form part of a meaningful display.

- Ask people to sign a book as they arrive, or even write a few sentences.

It can be a fabulous memory to have a hand-written record of those that attended a funeral, especially in the years to come. Depending on the general makeup of the mourners, you may wish to consider asking people to write a longer entry. Some may even take a few minutes to write something that could be read out during the funeral.

During the Service

- Close friends and family could place single flowers on the coffin.

Perhaps you will invite all mourners to do so, especially if you have a good idea as to how many will attend. It may be awkward to not have enough flowers for all those that want to take part.

Sometimes people will simply be invited to file past a coffin, often laying a hand gently on the outside as they pass.

- Photographs and other personal items could be placed around the coffin or on display nearby.

After a viewing and in consultation with the Funeral Director, letters or small personal items may be placed in coffin just prior to closing, to remain with the deceased.

Photographs of the deceased person can be a very powerful image of happiness that was shared, and will remind us that there were many parts to a life that was lived.

- Candles can play a very important symbolic role in a funeral.

Traditionally a candle may represent life, or the life of a spirit that remains when we die. There are many variations as to how a candle may be used. Sometimes a single candle can be lit in memory, or sometimes we will choose to light many candles. Some traditions will light a candle near the end of a service to signify that hope and love always remain, and other traditions will require that the candle that has burned throughout the service be extinguished as a final farewell takes place.

- Music, art, photographs, hand-crafted items, poetry and other writings from the person that died can form an important part of a meaningful funeral.

When we find a way to use the personal examples of somebody's creativity, we are often getting very close to finding a window through which we can gain a glimpse of their spirit or soul.

If your loved one devoted time to creative pursuits, think about including this special part of their personality in the funeral.

After the Service

- The release of butterflies or birds can be a wonderful way of "setting free the spirit" and allowing those present at a funeral to participate in a practical way to creating memories.

In recent years companies have emerged that supply these services, with great consideration to the treatment of the creatures that they release. For example, the natural habitat of the release area is considered, to ensure the comfortable transition of the particular species of butterfly or bird to be released.

- Helium balloons are also a choice for releasing after a funeral.

They can provide a spectacular and moving display of colour as they are released to follow the breeze. Some people, however, are concerned for the environmental impact as the balloons as they eventually land and settle.

- If you really want to create a feeling of "celebrating a life lived", then there are many ways to do this in a truly individual or memorable way.

Families have let off fireworks, staged a concert, cooked a traditional feast, delighted in displays of skydiving, motorbike parades, fire truck water fountains, ceremonial church bells, and many other experiences.

You know the person that died. What would they have particularly approved of? What would they have particularly enjoyed?

Memorials

It is worth considering any plans you may already have for a memorial in the weeks ahead. Perhaps there is something that you need to do, either prior to or during the funeral, to ensure that your memorial can go ahead.

Look ahead to the information on Memorials in the next section 'After the Funeral' if you think this may apply to you.

Technology and Creating Memories

Although some people are still unsure about the idea, the use of technology in memorial gatherings is rapidly bringing a powerful change in the ways we can choose remember a loved one.

There are three main areas in which we can consider the use of technology –

To recreate the memory of the person who died

Photographs and other memorabilia displayed at a gathering can be wonderful, but consider turning these photographs into a DVD movie. It could be played silently as people arrive and leave, or even form a central part of the memorial with accompanying music.

There are many computer programs available now that allow us to create good quality "movies" in our own homes. Somebody in your family may be very enthusiastic about contributing in this way, or there are also reputable companies that can create this for you professionally and at short notice.

Usually around 60 photographs can be scanned and placed to a piece of music to create a very powerful display of your loved one's life.

Recordings of favourite songs can be very quickly and inexpensively obtained through the internet.

If you have a recording of the deceased's voice, perhaps even as part of a home movie, listen right through the recording. You may well find some words that are fitting for the occasion, or even just typical of what they would say. As babies waiting to be born, we can still recognise the sound of voices belonging to people we have not yet met in person. It is possibly the most powerful reminder of someone that we will ever have.

Their memory will always live on in our hearts, and even if you think it may be painful, consider letting their voice live on as well.

To help us remember the memorial gathering and those that attended

Many people travel through the first few days and weeks following a death in a state of shock and unreality. Although we are aware that we were comforted by the presence of friends and family, it is often months or years later that we wish we could truly remember the words and actions that took place.

Consider asking somebody to use a digital camera on the day – you can take as many photos as you please, and discard at a later date (without wasting any money) those that are unsuccessful or inappropriate. Digital format allows us to email those that could not attend, choose which photographs to print, or crop photographs to a more suitable image. Digital photographs can easily and quickly be transferred onto a memorial tribute or thankyou card to be sent after the funeral.

Although not usually considered appropriate, it can sometimes be an excellent idea to consider a video / DVD camera recording.

No longer just for the rich or famous, video footage of the funeral can help us easily recreate both a cherished memory and powerful event in shaping our future. You may conduct "interview" style filming of those that attend, or you may just discretely record the events before, during or after without any particular sounds attached.

As a DVD recording also records the audio sound, you may feel comfortable allowing a video camera into the actual memorial. Eulogies, singing, words of comfort and love that are spoken – all these can be very powerful in the months and years ahead. If you are not comfortable with the visual record, simply move the sounds onto a CD recording.

To bring closer those that cannot attend in person

Copies of CDs played, digital photographs and DVD movie recordings can be easily emailed or downloaded from anywhere in the world with internet access. Some people will choose to join or start a memorial website to further perpetuate the memory of a loved one, providing access to memories at all times for those that want to log in.

A very exciting development is the use of web-cams to provide "virtual" attendance for someone who cannot attend in person. Perhaps you are able to stream instantaneously using Skype or similar programs, or perhaps you may store the broadcast digitally with the service provider for many months.

There are many internet "communities" that come together through chat rooms. Although we are all unique, it can be very comforting to find others who are sharing your experiences. You may be very surprised in the universal nature of our grief, and our common need to listen or be listened to.

The realisation that technology is allowing us to remember as never before is something that many families are very quickly embracing.

Seeking Greater Meaning

Some people are able to find purpose in a death, and it is very possible that the dead can help the living in this way.

If a death is unexpected or traumatic, or of a young or vulnerable person, then we can be especially challenged to try to make sense of what has happened. Many of our greatest and most inspired moments occur at times of extreme stress – when we are forced to evaluate exactly what is important and how best we might spend our remaining days in this life.

It is not unusual to want to honour the memory of somebody at a funeral by focussing on the cause of death and speaking out to warn or rally others to try to prevent the sad event from occurring again in the future. Examples include those that die through drink driving, drug use, mental illness or many other misfortunes. Also included are those that have died from a disease for which we believe a cure may be found someday.

Many people decide to ask mourners to consider donating to a relevant charity or research organisation, so that the gathering may feel that the person had "not died in vain" and perhaps through their death something can be contributed to the common good of all.

There are many possibilities
for creating a meaningful funeral
and memorial, and further ideas
are contained throughout this book.

Set aside some time to imagine,
time to consider or reflect,
and see what you come up with.

Sometimes we are truly able to honour someone best when we use our life as a memorial.

If we know that a loved one would want
to see us happy and living our lives with
purpose and grace, then we can strive
to do this in the best way we can.

Chapter 12 After the Funeral

In the days following a funeral, try to gently balance the demands of modern life with your responsibility to look after yourself. There are often many things still to do, and many decisions still to make. Most of these financial and legal details can wait, at least a day or two, while you pause to gather your strength.

Keep busy, but don't push yourself. Be independent, but allow others to help. Take things as they come, and resist the temptation to look too far ahead. You are still travelling through grief, and the road is never straight or simple to navigate.

Remember to Say "Thankyou"

There will be many people that have helped you and will continue to help you in the time ahead.

When we think of others, we are temporarily transported from our own sadness into a feeling of gratefulness, of trust, and of hope.

Many cultures have the saying "It is better to give than receive." We can feel helpless and powerless when somebody dies, but it is still possible to accept help graciously, and not lose a sense of who we are. All things have a time, and now is your time to receive. Some people may be very uncomfortable with this. You may need to actively set about letting others know that you will be ok, that you appreciate all that they are doing for you, and that some day you will be strong enough to return the favour.

If you are able to, it is a good idea to consider putting together a list of people that you may wish to thank. You could send a card to those that attended the funeral, or helped you to organise catering, or perhaps somebody just managed to do the right thing at exactly the right time.

Everybody that you have been in contact with the last few days knows that you are grateful. They do not expect you do to anything, and perhaps you will simply not be up to communicating your feelings.

If this is the case, do not feel pressured. People helped you because they want to; they would do anything they can to relieve your sadness at this time.

The best thankyou is for you to do what you need to do – whatever allows you to move through your grief.

Financial and Legal Considerations

There may be many financial and legal considerations to attend to when someone dies. Depending on their age and relationship to you, it may mean that the decisions and paperwork of the last few days are only part of the many things you must attend to when someone dies.

It does not help to list here all the possible organisations and details that may need your attention in the next few weeks. The list would be far too long, and probably mostly irrelevant to your particular circumstances. It could seem overwhelming and impossible to complete.

Attending to financial and legal considerations is one area where it is definitely an advantage to enlist the help of others. Contact a trusted friend, relative or professional advisor and allow them to help you.

It can be very upsetting to be telephoning or writing for hours, constantly retelling the death of your loved one. There are certain things that only you can authorise or sign, and you will have to be very involved at many levels along the way. But just as busy or stressed executives have a personal secretary, you should do the same.

Many organisations will need a copy of the Death Certificate, and will then complete the changes required for you and follow up with some new paperwork for you to sign. Some countries have government departments that are interlinked, and will be able to make many of the changes you need from one central authority.

You should expect everybody you deal with to be sympathetic at this time, and do not get upset if you find difficult individuals along the way. Simply call back later, or get someone else to deal with the complications for you.

Some of the possible organisations and people that may need your attention –

Legal	Registration of Death Reading and Enacting of a Will Joint ownership of assets (house, shares, car etc)
Financial	Funeral Directors and associated services Banking Accounts Government assistance or pensions Work related contracts
Community	Sporting or Cultural groups Health Care

Keep a clear list of –

- *Who* you have made contact with

The organisation and the name of the person you dealt with

- *When* this was done

Include the date, time, and remember to list each time you made contact

- Any *follow up* details you may need to attend to

This could include if they are sending you forms, or if you need to wait for other details to be completed first.

Now is not the time to rely on your memory. If others are helping you, they will need an accurate record of where you are up to in each transaction.

Your Funeral Director can be an excellent source of information and assistance in getting you started. They will often have the ability to organise some matters for you, or have a list of contact details for your national or local area.

Memorials

A memorial is a focus for reflection and a permanent marker for a life lived. Family, friends and unknown future generations can come to a specific location to remember and pay respects to their heritage.

You may have already decided on how and where you wish to place a memorial to your loved one. There is no need to hurry this decision, and you may well find that you will feel differently in the weeks or even months ahead.

It is perfectly usual for a memorial to become more important as time goes on. Many families have decided to place a memorial decades after the death of someone. Other families will restore a memorial centuries old. We can never know the ways in which a memorial may be significant in the time to come.

Traditional Memorial

If you have chosen a traditional burial or will place ashes in a dedicated area, then you will need to decide on the style and wording of the memorial.

Some areas may use a metal or stone memorial, and the variations available are great. It can take many weeks for this to be produced, and there is no rush to complete your final tribute.

Remember to consider the surrounding memorials when you make your choice. It is respectful to both your family and the families surrounding you, and occasionally there will be a particular protocol or style to follow. If you are unsure, just ask.

Take your time, perhaps visit the area with a friend, and have a look around at what others have chosen.

There may be a clear cultural or religious tradition you wish to follow.

Perhaps a certain memorial appeals to you because of the theme or the way it was created. If you see one that particularly appeals, feel free to ask staff how and where it was created.

Many memorials are crafted by people that are proud of their traditions or creativity, and will be only to happy to discuss options with you.

There are no rules as to what legally constitutes a memorial. You are free to respectfully do whatever best suits you and your family.

No Memorial

Perhaps you have decided to scatter ashes in a specific location. Perhaps you have opted for a woodland burial with only a tree or plant as a marker.

You may decide at a later date to erect a memorial in memory of your loved one at this or another location, or to start a small book that contains details of where ashes were scattered so that others yet to be born may know. There is time to decide, and your feelings may change as time goes on.

Other Ideas

Discussions with friends and family, your Funeral Director, or an internet search will reveal many options for creating a memorial.

Some may be surprising or unusual, but rest assured that if there is a company that offers a particular product, then you will not be the first family to choose it!

Perhaps some of the following ideas will prompt your own unique way of remembering someone that has died.

Garden Seat

You will need to approach your local council for permission, but it can be surprising how supportive a community authority may be about erecting a seat with a memorial plaque attached in a public place.

Name a Star

Although you will not get to visit it, you will certainly get to see your star named in honour of a person that has died. A certificate is sent to you, recognising the official name.

Start a Foundation

Sometimes we are in position to offer financial support to organisations that need public funding to continue.

Donations could start at the funeral, and continue with fundraising events and other ideas to increase public awareness.

You could aim for a large foundation, supporting a community awareness or medical service, or simply a small annual scholarship in your loved one's honour.

Create a Reef

Some people are very enthusiastic about giving back to the natural world, and helping to create a reef offshore for fish and other marine life can be a very fitting tribute.

Jewellery and Ornaments

Ashes can be placed into many items tastefully by jewellers that are sympathetic to your request. This may be inappropriate for you to consider, or it may create a meaningful family heirloom to treasure.

Some companies can create candles with images on them, or perhaps you can engrave certain items with meaningful words.

Start or Join a Website

There are many sites dedicated to hosting your loved one's web page. Options range from simply placing words, photos and music for other to view, through to an interactive and ever-changing site that allows you and others to remember them in your daily lives and activities. Some sites are perpetually funded by charitable organisations to ensure they will always be available.

Create a "LifeBook"

Sometimes we need to gather photos, music, thoughts and other items into one place, in honour of a person that died. Perhaps we create a DVD and send copies to others, engage a writer to record in print a life story, or perhaps we decorate a wooden box and place precious memories inside. There are many possibilities for creating your own personal family memorial.

A Final Thought

Consider that sometimes we are truly able to honour someone best when we use our life as a memorial. If we know that a loved one would want to see us happy and living our lives with purpose and grace, then we can strive to do this in the best way we can.

Chapter 13 Grief Resources

It is beyond the scope of this book to cover all that needs to be said about grief and loss. We all have different personalities, and each death will find us in different circumstances from the one before.

You are not alone in your experiences, and now is not the time to "be strong" and resist your feelings. Accept help, have courage, and start to move through your grief. You do not have to travel this journey alone.

As well as traditional community sources such as doctors and health care professionals, mental health specialists, focus groups, government and private organisations, and of course our own friends and family, there are some excellent resources available through the internet.

Do not restrict your search to your own particular country. Grief is of course a universal experience, but each individual will find comfort in the different approaches offered through a wide variety of sources.

In addition to supplying information, there are many "chat rooms" that you can join or simply observe, and there are often links to real-life people and organisations that you can meet with or speak to over the phone. There is help available – reach out and you will find many others waiting to help you along.

These sites may provide a good starting point –

www.griefnet.org

www.grief.org.au

The information on the following pages was taken from www.caringinfo.org

Overview

Grief is how one reacts to a loss.

Grief reactions may be experienced in response to physical losses, such as a death or in the response to symbolic or social losses such as a divorce or loss of a job.

All loss involves the absence of someone loved or something that fulfils a significant need in one's life.

Grief may be experienced in the combination of mental, physical, or social reactions.

- Mental/emotional reactions can include anger, guilt, anxiety, sadness, and despair
- Physical reactions can include sleeping problems, changes in appetite, physical problems, or illness
- Social reactions can include feelings about taking care of others in the family, role changes in the family, returning to work, or differences in social situations.

There is no right or wrong way to grieve after a significant loss. Most discover how to eventually move on with life, even though the grief experience is a difficult and trying time.

Coping styles depend on one's personality and their relationship with the person who has died. This experience can also be affected by one's cultural and religious background, coping skills, mental history, and their support system.

Taking care of yourself, and accessing the support of friends and family, can help a person get through difficult times.

Bereavement

Bereavement is the period after a loss during which grief is experienced.

The time spent in a period of bereavement depends on how attached the person was to the person who died, and how much time was spent anticipating the loss.

Some view the process of bereavement as having 4 phases:

Shock and numbness

Usually occurring soon after a death, this is evident when the person finds it difficult to believe the death has occurred; is feeling stunned and numb.

Yearning and searching

As shock and numbness recede, there remains the tendency to "forget" the person has died. Perhaps one catches a glimpse of somebody who reminds them of the deceased, or you expect them to be there when you first arrive home.

Disorganisation and despair

As the reality of the absence of the person who died settles in, it is common to feel depressed and find it difficult to think about the future. You may be easily distracted, or have difficulty concentrating and focusing on any one task.

Reorganisation

As one slowly makes the adjustment to all the ways in his or her life that have changed as a result of the loss, a sense of reorganisation and renewal begins to evolve.

Life is forever changed after a significant loss, but you slowly learn how the different aspects of your life become reprioritised as you "pick up the pieces" and begin to move on.

It is not that you forget about the person who died, but you have begun to learn how to live with this knowledge.

Some Common Questions

What is grief?

Grief is the normal response of sorrow, emotion, and confused emotions that come from the loss of someone or something important to you.

It is a natural part of life.

Grief is a typical reaction to death, divorce, job loss, a move away from family and friends, or loss of good health due to illness.

How does grief feel?

Following a death or loss, you may feel empty and numb, as if you are in shock.

You may notice physical changes such as trembling, nausea, trouble breathing, muscle weakness, dry mouth, or trouble sleeping and eating.

You may become angry – at a situation, a particular person, or just angry in general.

Guilt is a common response which may be easier to accept and overcome by looking at the experience in terms of "regret". When we think "I regret I was not in the room when he died" or "I regret I was not able to speak more openly about dying" it is less critical than "I feel guilty about my behaviour".

People in grief may have strange or disturbing dreams, be absent-minded, withdraw socially, or lack the desire to participate in activities that used to be enjoyable.

While these feelings and behaviours are normal during grief, they will pass.

How long does grief last?

Grief lasts as long as it takes you to accept and learn to live with your loss. For some people, this is a few months. For others, it may take years.

The length of time spent grieving is different for each person. There are many reasons for the differences, including personality, health, coping style, culture, family background, other stressors and life experiences.

The time spent grieving also depends on your relationship with the person lost and how prepared you were for the loss.

How will I know when I'm done grieving?

After a significant loss, you may be consumed and overwhelmed by the grief reactions you are experiencing.

In time, as the reality of the loss sinks in, and all the changes as a result of the loss have been experienced, you will learn to adjust to living without the physical presence of the person who died.

Eventually, even after significant loss, you will realize you are grieving less as you discover renewed energy in living. You will become less consumed by the impact of the loss and begin to draw comfort rather than pain from the memories. In a sense, you are never "done grieving."

With a significant loss, there will always be moments when you will remember the loss, and perhaps you experience some of the feelings of grief.

Fortunately, the time period between these surges will lengthen considerably as you learn how to cope with your loss.

Checklist of Arrangements

A brief summary of some alternatives to consider –

Burial or Cremation

We will gather at –

	(Before a service)
	(For a service)
	(At interment or burial)
	(Afterwards)

How we will let everybody know
(eg – newspaper, telephone, internet, notice at club or workplace)

Who will coordinate the replies if we ask people to notify they are attending

We will / will not hold a viewing, at location

The gathering will be led by

When we will meet to prepare with this person

Our Funeral Director will attend to the following details.
(eg – paperwork and liaison regarding death, cremation / burial, transport, flowers, placing newspaper notices, catering, music, printing, any other details)

Other people to be involved, and what they will do.
For example –
Speak
Read
Play or select music
Gather items to display
Organise or supply food or drink, including glasses or plates
Organise or provide transport
Attend to special items eg flowers, candles, photo displays, Order of Service printing

Recording Memories for Loved Ones

Perhaps you are reading this book with a view to your own funeral tribute. Or perhaps you have been planning the funeral of a loved one.

It is inevitable that when somebody dies our sense of history, of future, and of our own mortality is brought into the light and reassessed. Suddenly it can seem that we need to put things in perspective. We need to move from our daily lives into a much broader and universal view of our existence. We need to tell our story, and we want to sit by the camp-fire and listen to the story of others.

Consider putting down your memories and thoughts on paper. Just a simple collection of words can mean so much to others as time goes on. Many of the draft-readers of this book found themselves motivated to do exactly that.

Make notes, scribble thoughts, draw a childish picture, list items in order or complete random, even quote your favourite people, songs, movies or books. You may wish to write comments that attach to certain photos, or talk into a microphone for a while.

Don't think that others know all there is to know about you. Your personal notes will state your point of view, not their personal interpretation.

You may find as you complete the following details that you are reminded of many things. These could included –

- Feelings and senses (smells, sounds, foods, habits and routines, new experiences and many other things)
- People and their habits, favourite phrases and activities
- Minor parts of your life "When I think of the weekends, I think of..."
- Major parts of your life "The turning point came the day that..."

Do not disregard any emotion or memory you have as trivial. If it comes to mind first, then it is an important memory. Write it down, in whatever form you choose.

If you like to take your time, then it may suit you to write a little each day.

Most people cannot possibly write a beautifully crafted novel-length memoir without professional assistance, and even then you will have missed out so many details.

Just enjoy yourself and get started!

You don't need to pass on wisdom or stunning insights, that is the job of intellectual philosophers.

You do need to pass on a sense of who you were, who you have become, and the thoughts, actions, circumstances and beliefs that have carved you into the wonderfully unique you.

You have not lived alone, you are important, and others (perhaps even those you have not yet met) will thank you for your thoughtfulness from the bottom of their heart.

Take the time to record yourself.
It will be worth it.
You may even surprise yourself!

My Full Name, Place and date of Birth

My parents, brothers and sisters, and other comments about my schooling and where I grew up

My early adulthood was a time of...

I am most proud of...

I regret...

If I could live to be 200 years old, I would spend the rest of that time...

Bibliography

Title	Author	Publisher / Year
Funeral & Memorial Service Readings, Poems & Tributes	Baum, Rachel (Ed)	McFarland 1999
Psychosocial Aspects of Death and Dying	Canine	McGraw-Hill 1996
Complete Guide to Funeral Planning: How to Arrange the Appropriate Service	Carnell	Lyons Press 2005
World Religions	Catoir	St Pauls 1992, update 2003
Simply Essential Funeral Planning Kit	Cochrane	Self Counsel Press 2002
Remember Me: A Lively Tour of the New American Way of Death	Cullen	Harper Collins 2006
Music is the Voice of All Sorrow, All Joy	Exley	Exley Publications 1992
To Someone Special in Times of Trouble	Exley	Exley Publication 1999
Words of Comfort	Exley	Exley Publication 1999
At Journey's End: The Complete Guide To Funerals and Funeral Planning	Fatteh, Abdullah & Naaz	Health Info 1999
Remembrances and Celebrations: A book of Eulogies, Elegies, Letters and Epitaphs	Harris, Jill (Ed)	Random House 1999
What to Do When Somebody Dies: How to deal with the Practical Arrangements that have to be Made after a Death	Harris	Which UK 2005

Christians Grieve Too	Howard, Donald	Banner of Truth UK USA 1979
Last Wishes: A Funeral Planning Manual & Survivors Guide	James & Lyn	Mavami 2000
How Different Religions View Death and Afterlife	Johnson et al	Charles Press 1998
Complete Book of Funeral Planning Readings & Music: How to plan and organise the funeral your loved ones would most appreciate	Johnstone, Gibbs & Wynburne	Foulsham 2005
On Death and Dying: What the dying have to teach doctors, nurses, clergy and their own families	Kubler-Ross	Scribner 1969
A Humanist Funeral Service	Lamont Corliss	Prometheus 1954, 1977
Saying Goodbye Your Way: Planning or Buying a Funeral or Cremation for Yourself or Someone You Love	Llewellyn, John	Tropico Press 2004
For Weddings and a Funeral: Special Poems for Special Occasions	Marsden, John	Pan McMillan 1996, 2006
Perfect Stranger's Guide to Funerals and Greiving Practices: A Guide to Etiquette in Other People's Religious Ceremonies	Matlins	Skylight Paths 2000
Dealing Creatively with Death	Morgan, Ernest	Upper Access 2001
Readings for Remembrance: A Collection for Funerals and Memorial Services	Munro, Eleanor (Ed)	Penguin Books 2000

In Memorium: A Guide to Modern Funeral and Memorial Services	Searl	Skinner House Books 2000
In Preparation: How to Have a Funeral	Shaw & Shaw	Readsome 2002
For My Family: A Legacy for Future Generations	Stone	New Holland 2004
Final Celebrations	Sublette & Flagg	Pathfinder 1992
Winning Ways: The Funeral Profession's Guide to Human Relations	Van Beck, Todd	Appleton 1999
Funerals Without God: A Practical Guide to Non-Religious Funerals	Wilson	Prometheus 1990
Creating Meaningful Funeral Ceremonies: A Guide for Families	Wolfelt	Companion Press 2000
Creating Meaningful Funeral Ceremonies: A Guide for Caregivers	Wolfelt	Companion Press 2003
Remembering Well: Rituals for Celebrating Life and Mourning Death	York, Sarah	Wiley 2000
Forever Remembered	Zadra & Woodard	Compendium Inc 2003

Copyright Permissions

We have made extensive efforts to contact the copyright holders of poetry and other quotations for 'When We Remember'. The publishers regret any omissions and would appreciate any opportunity to ask for permission and correctly acknowledge quoted authors in future editions.

"When You Are Old" by W.B.Yeats – Reprinted by kind permission of A.P.Watt on behalf of Grainne Yeats.

"Funeral Blues" by W.H.Auden – Reprinted by kind permission of Faber and Faber.

"Do Not Go Gentle Into That Good Night" by Dylan Thomas – Reprinted by kind permission of New Directions Publishing Group also David Higham Associates Ltd, London

"I'll Be There" by Maude Hurford – Printed by kind permission of Judy Wade

"My One True Thing" by Lyn Anderson – Printed by kind permission of the author

'When We Remember' Music CD

Instrumental Solos

Solo Piano	"Pathetique" Sonata 2nd Movement	Beethoven
	"Moonlight" Sonata 1st Movement	Beethoven
Solo Organ	"Jesu, Joy of Man's Desiring"	J S Bach
Solo Guitar	"Prelude No.1"	Villa-Lobos
Solo Bagpipe	Amazing Grace	Traditional
Solo Trumpet	Last Post and Reveille	Traditional

Instrumental Solos with Piano Accompaniment

Flute	"Pavanne"	Faure
Flute and Clarinet	"Sicillienne"	Faure
Cello	"The Swan" from Carnival of the Animals	Saint-Saëns
Violin	"Meditation" from Thais	Massenet

Solos with Organ or Other Accompaniment

Guitar and Strings	"Concerto de Aranjuez"	Rodrigo
Female Voice	"My Redeemer Liveth" from Messiah	Handel
	"Pie Jesu" from Requiem	Faure
Choir	"Ave Verum"	Mozart
String Quartet	"Adagio" in G minor	Albinoni
	"Canon"	Pachelbel
	"Air" from Suite No.3	J S Bach

'When We Remember' Accompanying CD Playlist

Music for Listening and Reflection

1	The Swan *from Carnival of the Animals*	Saint-Saens	2.55
2	Sicilienne	Faure	2.16
3	Concerto de Aranjuez	Rodrigo	3.00
4	Sonata "Pathetique" *2nd Movt*	Beethoven	3.22
5	Adagio in G minor	Albinoni	3.20
6	Pavanne	Faure	2.43
7	Prelude No.1	Villa-Lobos	1.58
8	Air *from Suite No.3*	J.S.Bach	4.08
9	Sonata "Moonlight" *1st Movt*	Beethoven	2.58
10	Meditation *from Thais*	Massenet	4.09
11	Pie Jesu *from Requiem*	Faure	2.45
12	Canon	Pachelbel	3.12
13	I Know My Redeemer Liveth *from Messiah*	Handel	2.25
14	Jesu, Joy of Man's Desiring	J.S.Bach	2.44
15	Ave Verum	Mozart	2.35

Music for Singing and Ceremony

16	The Lord is My Shepherd	Psalm 23 / Crimond	2.51
17	Going Home (Christ Gone Before)	Unknown / Dvorak	2.55
18	Abide With Me	Lyte / Monk	3.07
19	Going Home (Live in Me)	Abraham / Dvorak	2.48
20	Amazing Grace (Choir)	Traditional	3.10
21	Amazing Grace (Bagpipe)	Traditional	2.25
22	Last Post	Traditional	1.29
23	Reveille	Traditional	0.27

You will find your 'When We Remember' music CD inside the back cover of this book.